MW00436621

PERFECT IN CHRIST

THE GOOD NEWS OF GOD'S GRACE

MITCHELL C. TAYLOR
WITH CAMERON C. TAYLOR

Books by Cameron C. Taylor

8 Attributes of Great Achievers

8 Attributes of Great Achievers, Volume II

Preserve, Protect, & Defend

Does Your Bag Have Holes? 24 Truths That Lead to Financial and Spiritual Freedom

Twelve Paradoxes of the Gospel

8 Steps to Lasting Excellence

The Way of Aloha: Lana'i

The Way of Aloha: Moloka'i

Cameron's Website
www.CameronCTaylor.com

Library of Congress Control Number: 2020936146
ISBN-13: 978-0-9796861-8-4
Printed in the United States of America

This book is dedicated to Dr. Stephen E. Robinson. Thank you for teaching my dad the Good News so he could teach me.

TABLE OF CONTENTS

CHAPTER 1
RECEIVE CHRIST'S GRACE

"Man can only be saved by the grace of Jesus Christ."

- Chapter Heading for JST, Romans 4:2-5

When I was five years old, my dad was a scoutmaster. He and the scouts were working on the cinematography merit badge, and one of the scenes for the movie required a luxury car. Luckily, one of our neighbors, Dave Wilson, owned two beautiful Ferraris—a red one and a yellow one—and he was willing to allow the scouts to film a scene using them. My dad allowed me to tag along on the evening they went to Dave's home to film. As my dad and Dave visited, I, being a curious and energetic five-year-old, decided to explore the terrain. To my delight, I discovered a swivel chair to play with. I began spinning around and around on the chair. Unfortunately, the chair was located on an elevated workbench, directly above the red Ferrari. I was having a blast until both the swivel chair and I plummeted off the platform, landing directly on the hood of the Ferrari before finally falling to the floor below. As the ominous crash echoed through the garage, my dad and Dave apprehensively turned to see both the chair and my body sprawled on the ground.

As I glanced up from the ground, I knew my adventure with the chair had turned into a disaster. There were several dents and scratches on the hood of Dave's Ferrari. I immediately sprinted and took shelter behind my dad. My heart was racing, and I was frightened of my impending punishment. Dave walked toward my dad and attempted to talk with me, but in my panicked state, I couldn't understand anything he was saying. Clutching my dad's legs, I moved from side to side to avoid Dave's eyes. Dave quickly realized I was too terrified to speak with him directly, so he gently knelt near my dad and said,

"Don't worry about it, Mitchell. That is why they make paint. I will be able to have it fixed. Everything will be okay."

When we returned home that night, my dad sat me down and said, "Mitchell, I know that what you did was an accident, but you are still responsible for the damage you have caused tonight. I need you to get your piggy bank and give all of the money you have saved to Dave to help pay for the repair."

Tears began to well up in my eyes. "No, Dad, no," I pleaded. "I don't want to lose all my money. I don't want to start all over."

"Mitchell, when we damage something that does not belong to us, we have a responsibility and an obligation to pay to repair the damage," my dad replied.

After emptying every last penny I owned into an envelope, my dad took the package from my trembling hands and returned to Dave's home.

When Dave opened his front door, my father handed him the tear-stained envelope and said, "Dave, this envelope contains all of Mitchell's money, as well as a signed blank check. I am truly sorry for the damage we have caused to your car and want to make things right."

Without a moment of hesitation, Dave returned the envelope into my father's hands. "You are a man of honor, Cameron, but I can't take this."

"My son is responsible for the damage, Dave, so I want to pay to fix it. It's not fair for you to be responsible for something my son did."

"You don't need to worry about it," Dave said with kindness. "I will be able to have it repaired. Consider it a gift."

Dave extended forgiveness and grace to both my dad and me that night. He agreed to pay for the damage to his Ferrari that we were responsible for. Just as Dave lifted the burden of paying for the damage to the Ferrari, Christ has lifted the burden of sin from each of us through His atoning sacrifice in the Garden of Gethsemane and on the cross. The Lord declares, "Though your sins be as scarlet, they shall be as white as snow; though they be red like crimson, they shall be as wool... I will forgive... and I will remember [your] sin no more."[1]

Christ further declared, "For behold, I, God, have suffered these things for all, that they might not suffer if they would repent... Which suffering caused myself, even God, the greatest of all, to tremble because of pain, and to bleed at every pore, and to suffer both body and spirit."[2] Christ has already paid to repair the damage we cause each time we metaphorically scratch a Ferrari through our sins and mistakes in life. He has lovingly paid that debt for us with His own blood so we don't have to pay for it ourselves.

Although Dave extended grace and forgiveness to both me and my dad that night, I never actually knew about Dave's generous gift. After returning from Dave's home, my dad put my envelope of money in his closet. He wanted to teach me to take responsibility for my actions, so I never knew my debt had been forgiven and I didn't have to pay for the damage I had caused.

A year after this incident, my dad was writing a chapter on grace for one of his books. He was writing about how we often have a hard time accepting Christ's forgiveness and grace because we assume we don't deserve it and it doesn't seem fair. That is the whole point of grace, though. Christ is giving us something we don't deserve. If we deserved it, it wouldn't be grace. It would instead be a reward or a wage.

As my dad wrote about grace, his mind reverted to that evening the previous year in Dave's garage with the scratched Ferrari. He realized he was guilty of the very thing he was writing about. My dad was so focused on teaching me about fairness, justice, and the consequences of my actions that he missed a wonderful opportunity to teach me about grace and forgiveness.

A few days later, when our family gathered for a family night, my dad asked me if I remembered the incident with our neighbor's Ferrari. As soon as I heard the word "Ferrari," my face began to flush and my body tensed up. I drooped my head and whispered, "Please, Dad, I don't want to talk about that."

Gently raising my chin with his hand, my dad looked me in the eyes, smiled, and said, "You are going to like this story, Mitchell. I never told you what happened when I went to Dave's house with your money that night. When I offered to pay for the damage you caused to his Ferrari, Dave refused to accept your money. He said he would have the Ferrari repaired and the damage was forgiven as a gift."

I looked up at my dad with confusion in my eyes. What exactly was he saying? He then handed me an envelope. My eyes lit up with excitement as I felt the weight and heard the jingling of coins. My dad was giving my money back! I ripped the envelope open and began to count my newly acquired fortune. The anguish and shame I had felt from that night were replaced with joy and excitement.

A few years ago, my dad gave a talk in a sacrament meeting where he shared the Ferrari story and what we had learned from it. The following is an excerpt from his message:

> *When I sin, I am at times initially hesitant to go to the Lord and ask for forgiveness. I have a natural tendency to want to hide as Mitchell did after he scratched our neighbor's Ferrari and as Adam and Eve did after they partook of the forbidden fruit. Moses 4:14 reads, "And they heard the voice of the Lord God, as they were walking in the garden... and Adam and his wife went to hide themselves from the presence of the Lord God."*
>
> *When I sin, Satan and the natural man work to convince me that if I go to the Lord with my sins, the response from the Lord will be one of disappointment, condemnation, and alienation. Satan will put thoughts into my head such as, "You screwed up again. Do you really think the Lord will forgive you for the 432nd time? You are a failure. You are never going to change, so why try? Just give up." or "Hide, so you do not have to experience the disappointment and wrath of the Lord."*
>
> *You'd think I would have learned, both from my own previous encounters with the Lord seeking forgiveness and from examples in the scriptures, that this is not the case. The scriptures are filled with stories of Christ's mercy and forgiveness. The prophet Nehemiah describes Christ as "A God ready to pardon, gracious and merciful, slow to anger, and of great kindness."[3]*

Even though I know this, I still find that I have to fight the tendency to hide from the Lord when I do something wrong. Eventually, I get up the courage to go to the Lord in prayer and ask for forgiveness. Each time I petition the Lord in prayer for forgiveness, I am overwhelmed by His outpouring of love, acceptance, and forgiveness.

Moroni 6:8 reads, "As oft as they repented and sought forgiveness, with real intent, they were forgiven." And in the Doctrine and Covenants the Lord declares, "He who has repented of his sins, the same is forgiven, and I, the Lord, remember them no more."[4]

The book of 1 John states, "If we say that we have no sin, we deceive ourselves, and the truth is not in us. If we confess our sins, [Christ] is faithful and just to forgive us our sins...and the blood of Jesus Christ...cleanseth us from all sin."[5]

As we petition the Lord for forgiveness, we will hear the glorious words of the Savior, which He repeated many times during His earthly ministry, "Be of good cheer; thy sins be forgiven thee."[6]

As my father prepared his talk, he felt a clear prompting from God that this message was intended for a specific individual that day. The name of the individual was not revealed to him, though. As he spoke, he scanned the congregation, looking for whom he thought the intended recipient might be. Curiously, none of the individuals that came to his mind were present in the audience that morning.

After the meeting concluded, my dad walked past the stake president's office. President Summers, a counselor in the stake presidency, motioned him into the room.

"Are you the one who gave the talk about the Ferrari?" he asked.

"Yes," my father replied.

Our stake president, Mike Poston, who was also in the office, then said, "There was a man in the foyer waiting to talk with me this morning. As he waited, he heard your talk. He came into my office crying. As he told me about your talk, he said, 'The Lord has forgiven me. For the first time in my life, I feel forgiven.'"

"God told me my message was for a specific individual," my dad began, "but I couldn't figure out who God had in mind. All of the people I thought this talk might be for weren't at church today."

President Summers replied, "Your talk was for this man."

As President Summers spoke, the Spirit confirmed this truth to my father. The Lord knew this man would be in the foyer during our sacrament meeting. The Lord wanted this man to receive His forgiveness and grace. The Ferrari story and the scriptures that were shared opened the door for the Lord to pour His love, grace, and forgiveness into this man.

Even though Christ has forgiven our debt of sin, many of us either don't know we are forgiven or don't feel we are forgiven. We still suffer guilt for past mistakes. In my experience with the Ferrari, my dad hid my money with the intent to teach me that I had to pay for my mistakes. The reality, though, was that my debt was already paid in full. I didn't need to pay the debt because someone had paid it for me. We often do the same thing with our sins. We resist Christ's grace and forgiveness and try to pay for the debt of sin ourselves. Like me, we don't know our debt has been forgiven. Dave forgave me for damaging his Ferrari, but I didn't know this. Whenever someone would bring up the scratched Ferrari, I would start to cry. I was still embarrassed and humiliated by my mistake. When my dad returned my money, I finally received the grace and forgiveness Dave had extended to me the year before. My sadness and pain were quickly replaced with joy and gratitude.

In Elder Neil L. Andersen's talk, *Repent... That I May Heal You*, he states, "Being disciples of Christ, we rejoice in the blessing of repenting and the joy of being forgiven... Divine forgiveness is one of the sweetest fruits of the gospel, removing guilt and pain from our hearts and replacing them with joy and peace of conscience."

Now that is Good News!

CHAPTER 2
ARE YOU GOING TO THE CELESTIAL KINGDOM?

"Your sins are forgiven you; you are clean before me; therefore, lift up your heads and rejoice."[7]

- Jesus Christ

I have been blessed to grow up in a home with a dad who writes books on the Good News of the Lord Jesus Christ. I have been taught about forgiveness, grace, and salvation since I was little. I am now seventeen years old, and I have noticed many of my friends, church teachers, and local church leaders don't understand some of the doctrines of the gospel of Jesus Christ that I have been taught. I have had countless discussions with friends and church teachers about the doctrines of grace and salvation. More often than not, I leave these discussions saddened by the realization that many of my friends and teachers who go to church every week don't know about the Good News of Jesus Christ and therefore haven't received it.

I wanted to write this book to share the Good News with my friends. As I discussed with my dad how to write a book on the Good News of Jesus Christ, he suggested that we look at the results of a survey he has conducted with members of The Church of Jesus Christ of Latter-day Saints over the past two decades. This simple, two-question survey, which was completed by over one hundred faithful members who attend church each week in several Idaho and Utah wards, was designed to see what people believe about their salvation. Below are the questions on the survey:

Survey Questions

#1. Do you want to go to the celestial kingdom?
Circle one: Yes or No

#2. If you were to die today, at the resurrection would you go to the celestial kingdom?
Circle one: Yes   or   No   or   I don't know

Explain Why or Why Not?

The answers to the first question were not surprising. One hundred percent of the individuals surveyed answered identically. "Yes!" They all wanted to go to the celestial kingdom. The results to the second question were not unanimous, however, and these answers mirrored my personal experience regarding my own friends. Too many active members of The Church of Jesus Christ of Latter-day Saints don't know the Good News of Jesus Christ. Of those surveyed, 48 percent answered, "I don't know" to the question about whether they were going to the celestial kingdom. Only 30 percent of respondents answered, "Yes" to this question. Even though 100 percent of the individuals who took the survey wanted to go to the celestial kingdom, only 30 percent knew what was required to get there.

Although these numbers are insightful, the real key to understanding these survey results is not found in the percentage of yes and no answers that were given. True understanding is revealed in the explanations given by each individual as to why he or she answered yes or no on the survey as well as the implications that can be drawn from these responses.

Throughout the remainder of this book, I will analyze the various explanations given by those surveyed, identifying the truths that lead to a correct understanding of Christ's grace as well as incorrect beliefs that lead us to distorted beliefs about the Good News of Jesus Christ.

Let's begin by looking at the explanations given by those who answered, "Yes! I am going to the celestial kingdom." The following are actual answers from the survey:

"Because of the Savior Jesus Christ."

"I am in a covenant relationship with Christ."

"I have faith in Christ that through His atonement I will be cleansed and be able to enter the celestial kingdom."

"I know that my Savior's grace is sufficient."

"Although I am far from perfect, I know that it is through Christ I can be saved."

"By Christ's mercy."

"Through Christ and covenants."

"I know the Savior's promise is true."

"I have made and kept my covenants."

"I am on the path."

Of the 30 percent who answered in the affirmative that they were going to the celestial kingdom, all wrote about their covenant relationship with Jesus Christ and that Christ's mercy and grace were the source of their salvation. These individuals understand how they are saved! Two doctrines that are critical to the understanding of our covenant relationship with Jesus Christ are the doctrines of justification and sanctification. A great illustration to teach these two pivotal doctrines is what my dad likes to call the pit of sin.

The Pit of Sin

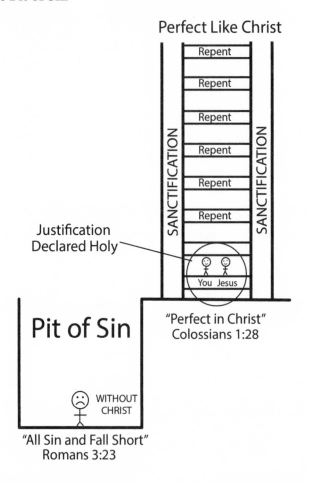

Pretend for a moment that you have fallen into a pit that is a mile deep. You try to climb the walls, but it's impossible. The walls of the pit go straight up and there is nothing to hold on to. You try jumping. You try climbing. You try digging. Each attempt you make to climb the wall results in the same outcome. You're falling back to the bottom of the pit.

As a result of the fall of Adam, we have all sinned and thus fall short of the perfection required to be in the presence of God. Spiritually, we have each fallen into the equivalent of a mile-deep pit. We try as hard as we can to overcome our fallen natures and to get right with God. We try to keep all the commandments, but since we inevitably fail, we then try to make it up to God by increasing our good works quota, hoping maybe these actions will sway the judgment of God in our favor. We hope somehow if our good works outweigh our sins, we will be able to get right with God. The bad news, though, is even after all of our disciplined efforts and our countless good works, we are still far from being perfect, and we are thus unable to escape the pit of sin.

As we begin to realize the futility of our situation, and that it is truly impossible to get ourselves out of this spiritual pit, we fall into despair. We so badly want to escape. All of our attempts lead us to a vital moment in which we turn to God and say as did the publican, "God be merciful to me a sinner."[8] We change from being confident in our own efforts to a state in which we leave it to God and recognize our total dependence upon Him.

As we glance up, we see Christ, arms outstretched, calling us by name. We cry out, "Lord, save me!"[9] Christ grabs us, pulling us out of the pit of sin, freeing us from its grasp.

Jesus Christ declares, "Come unto me, all ye that labour and are heavy laden, and I will give you rest. Take my yoke upon you... and ye shall find rest unto your souls. For my yoke is easy, and my burden is light... Come unto me [and] ye shall have eternal life.

Behold, mine arm of mercy is extended towards you, and whosoever will come, him will I receive… Come unto me… and be saved."[10]

In response to the Master's invitation, we yoke ourselves with Him, and instantly we are freed from the pit. Becoming one with Christ is the beginning of our life as a Christian. Being freed from the pit of sin by Christ is called justification. Through justification, we are declared not guilty and are made perfect in the eyes of God.

Justification

"We know that justification through the grace of our Lord and Savior Jesus Christ is just and true."
Doctrine and Covenants 20:30

In Stephen Robinson's book, *Believing Christ*, he compares our union with Christ to a marriage. He states, "As husband and wife become one with each other through the covenant of marriage, so the Savior and the saved become one with each other through the covenant of the gospel. Just as a bride renounces all competing claims upon her loyalties and normally takes her husband's name, so those who enter this covenant with Christ renounce all competing loyalties, put Him first, and take His name upon them. To this union, we bring our righteous desires and our loyalty. He brings His perfection. In the covenant union, what is mine becomes His, and what is His becomes mine. Thus, my sins become His for payment, and His righteousness becomes mine for justification. When we become one with Jesus Christ, spiritually we form a partnership with a joint account, and His assets and our liabilities flow into each other. Since He has more assets than we have liabilities, the new account has a positive balance as soon as it is formed, and the partnership is justified, even though its junior partners (you and me) could not make it on their own. This is what the Apostle Paul refers to as being 'in Christ' and what Moroni calls being 'perfect in Christ' (Moroni 10:32)."[11]

We are married to Christ through the ordinance and covenant of baptism. We become one with Christ and are judged according to His merits. We know Christ is perfect and holy without spot, so as we are judged by His merits, we can rest assured we are in a saved condition before the Father. As a result of this new relationship, we are justified and freed from the pit of sin instantly. Justification doesn't mean we suddenly become perfectly obedient and stop sinning. It means as sinners, we can still be declared righteous and perfect, not because we are perfect but because we are one with Christ, and He is righteous and perfect.

Elder D. Todd Christofferson explains justification in the following way: "[Christ] removes our condemnation without removing the law. We are pardoned and placed in a condition of righteousness with Him. We become, like Him, without sin… We are, in a word, justified."[12]

The requirement to be justified in Christ is not obedience but a true and sincere desire to become such through Christ. The Lord requires a broken heart and a contrite spirit.

Christ does not say, "Climb as far as you can and then I will take you the rest of the way." He says, "Climb onto my back, and I will free you from the pit of sin." Christ says, "Come unto me… and be saved."[13] To enter the covenant relationship with Christ requires our heart. Doctrine and Covenants 64:34 states, "Behold, the Lord requireth the heart and a willing mind." Justification requires that we want Christ to give us eternal life and we want to do what He asks of us.

Complete obedience is not required to enter the covenant of baptism, but is perfect obedience required to stay in our covenant with Christ? The answer is a resounding no! If perfect obedience were a requirement to remain in a covenant relationship with Christ, we would never be able to be in a relationship with Him since we continually sin. Through justification, we are instantly perfect in Christ, even though a gap remains between our actual performance and personal perfection. For obedience to be a requirement in order to be in a covenant relationship with Christ would mean we would have to be perfect before we could be justified, which defeats the entire purpose of justification.

This would be the equivalent to saying, "I know you are in a mile-deep pit that is impossible for you to get out of by yourself, but I can't help you until you can get yourself out of the pit. As soon as you can get out of the pit, I will come into the pit and take you to safety." God does not justify the righteous but the ungodly.[14] Christ declares, "They that are whole have no need of the physician, but they that are sick: I came not to call the righteous, but sinners to repentance."[15] The Apostle Paul declares, "Christ Jesus came into the world to save sinners; of whom I am chief."[16]

We all are imperfect, "For all have sinned and fall short of the glory of God,"[17] and "no unclean thing can dwell with God."[18] We cannot inherit the celestial kingdom on our own. Christ is the only way we can inherit eternal life in the celestial kingdom. The miracle of justification declares the imperfect as perfect in Christ and heirs of the celestial kingdom.

Sanctification

"We know also, that sanctification through the grace of our Lord and Savior Jesus Christ is just and true."

Doctrine and Covenants 20:31

Once we have experienced the instantaneous gift of justification, we begin the process of sanctification. "To be sanctified through the blood of Christ is to become clean, pure, and holy. If justification removes the punishment for past sin, then sanctification removes the stain or effects of sin."[19]

"Justification and sanctification both come by God's gracious will. Yet they are different things. Justification is a single act whereby God graciously declares the ungodly person not guilty instantly. Sanctification is a continual process whereby God graciously changes a believer's habits and behavior into holy deeds… The former is instantaneous; the latter is progressive. The persons on whom the blessing of sanctification is bestowed are those who are justified. Holiness is a wonderful blessing of the new covenant, not a condition to our entry into that covenant."[20]

As we enter a covenant relationship with Christ, we place our faith in Him to save us. When we have faith in Jesus Christ, we want to do the things He asks us to do. We trust Him. Some have foolishly declared, "'Faith is all that matters. Consequently, if you have faith, it doesn't matter what you do. Sin away, my lad, and have a good time and Christ will see that it makes no difference in the end.' The answer to that nonsense is that, if what you call your 'faith' in Christ does not involve taking the slightest notice of what He says, then it is not Faith at all."[21]

The apostle James declared, "I will shew thee my faith by my works."[22] The apostle Paul similarly taught, "What then? shall we sin, because we are not under the law, but under grace? God forbid."[23] If we believe God is our creator and place our faith in Him, we will also believe that His words are the best source for directing our lives.

The true doctrine of justification by grace does not lead to moral irresponsibility, laziness, passivity, or disobedience. True justification will never lead a man to more sin but will instead lead to fuller repentance and obedience. If you don't desire obedience (notice I have said desire, not that you are actually obedient), you haven't truly entered the covenant which justifies.

Sanctification is the process of aligning our actions with our desire for obedience. We obtain sanctification by repenting. It is the process of moving to a higher and higher level of obedience. Repentance is the process by which we improve and become more like Christ. Repentance is not an act of going from being a sinner to becoming obedient. We will not attain perfect obedience in this life. Thus, we are always disobedient. Repentance just diminishes the level of disobedience. The process of seeking to become more like Christ is what the scriptures refer to as enduring to the end. Matthew 24:13 declares, "He that shall endure unto the end, the same shall be saved."

What does it mean to endure to the end? Well, what is the end we are seeking? The end we desire is perfection and eternal life in the celestial kingdom. Often the scriptural use of the word *endure* means to continue rather than to suffer. Thus, enduring to the end can be understood to mean continuing toward perfection as we seek to fulfill the command to "Be ye therefore perfect, even as your Father which is in heaven is perfect."[24]

The journey of striving to become like Christ will last a lifetime. Every day God wants you to become a little more like Him. Colossians 3:10 declares, "You have begun to live the new life, in which you are being made new and are becoming like the One who made you."[25] Some may seek a way to instantly possess all the attributes of godliness, but growth is a process. Growth is gradual. The Bible says, "Our lives gradually [become] brighter and more beautiful as God enters our lives and we become like him."[26]

When Christ frees us from the pit of sin, we are instantly perfect in Him, but we are not instantly perfect like Him. Attaining complete obedience through Christ (sanctification) is a lengthy process. There are no shortcuts. Once we have escaped the pit of sin and are declared perfect in Christ, Christ leads us up the ladder of sanctification. Climbing this sanctification ladder is the process of becoming perfect like Christ. Our ascent up the ladder will often be slow, and at times we will fail and fall a few rungs. During these times, though, Christ will be there to catch us and help us begin our climb again. As we climb, we can have a perfect assurance that although we are not perfect like Christ, we are still perfect in Him.

While justification is instantaneous, the sanctification process will take a long, long time. We become more like Christ, "line upon line, precept upon precept, here a little and there a little."[27] Joseph

Smith taught, "When you climb up a ladder, you must begin at the bottom, and ascend step by step, until you arrive at the top; and so it is with the principles of the Gospel—you must begin with the first, and go on until you learn all the principles of exaltation. But it will be a great while after you have passed through the veil before you will have learned them. It is not all to be comprehended in this world; it will be a great work to learn our salvation and exaltation even beyond the grave."[28] Eventually, through the process of sanctification, "We shall become mature people, reaching to the very height of Christ's full stature."[29]

Conclusion

Elder D. Todd Christofferson teaches the doctrines of justification and sanctification this way. "Perfection is not, as some suppose, a prerequisite for justification and sanctification. It is just the opposite: justification (being pardoned) and sanctification (being purified) are the prerequisites for perfection. We only become perfect 'in Christ,' not independently of Him. Thus, what is required of us in order to obtain mercy in the day of judgment is simple diligence… The Savior offers to all who will have faith and accept it, the gifts of being justified or pardoned before the law and also being sanctified— that is, being made spotless and holy. There is no other name, nor way, nor means whereby such redemption may occur. And truly His grace is sufficient to achieve it."[30]

How were 30 percent of the survey respondents able to answer, "Yes! I am going to the celestial kingdom?" They could answer in the affirmative because they understand how they are saved. They know "redemption cometh in and through the Holy Messiah; [who] is full of grace and truth."[31] Christ is the only source for salvation. The Book of Mormon declares, "There is no other way or means whereby man can be saved, only in and through Christ."[32]

Christ declares, "Your sins are forgiven you; you are clean before me; therefore, lift up your heads and rejoice."[33]

Now that is Good News!

CHAPTER 3

WITH CHRIST, YOU ARE GOOD ENOUGH

"No flesh...can dwell in the presence of God, save it be through the merits, and mercy, and grace of the Holy Messiah."

- 2 Nephi 2:8

In my life, I have been able to attend many of my dad's presentations and watch him teach others. While I was at one of his presentations on his new book, *The Way of Aloha: Moloka'i*, I was enriched by what he was teaching, but my thoughts began to waver as he told us who the book was dedicated to. My dad's book is dedicated to one of his best friends, Mitch Huhem, who committed suicide while my dad was working on the book. My dad read from the book dedication, "This book is dedicated to Mitch Huhem, my friend, my mentor, my kahuna (expert), and my kumu (teacher). I learned from him how to be an instrument in the hands of the Lord in business and in life. He is a man full of love, generosity, happiness, and vision. Mitch, your positive influence continues in my life and the lives of my children. I will be eternally grateful for your love, example, generosity, life, and faith in me. As you know, my oldest son is named after you. I hope he grows up to become like the Mitch Huhem I know—the mighty man of God who I am blessed to call my friend."

While my dad was reading this, I began to cry. I thought, *I could never be half of the man Mitch was. I will never be good enough.* Immediately after I had uttered these words under my breath, the Holy Spirit told me, "If you continue on the path you are on and you stay with Jesus, you will be a mighty man of God." After I heard this voice, I was filled with peace and knew Jesus had a plan for me to become a mighty instrument in His hands.

Satan continually tells us, "You are not good enough." I am not alone in my thoughts of inadequacy. The most common explanation given by the survey respondents as to why they weren't going to the celestial kingdom were statements related to not being good enough. The following are actual responses:

"I am not good enough."

"I make a lot of mistakes."

"I have too many weaknesses to list."

"I am not worthy."

"I try to be a good person and have love for others, but sometimes I feel so unworthy and I know I lack Christlike qualities."

"Because I keep making mistakes."

"I don't know if I am that good, or worthy enough."

"Maybe I haven't done enough."

"I could always do better."

"I'm not doing everything I should be."

"I have anger issues."

Am I Good Enough?

The criterion these individuals were using to determine if they were going to the celestial kingdom was, "Am I good enough?" This can be seen in the pronouns these individuals chose to use in their statements. Notice the use of the pronoun "I" in each response:

"**I** make a lot of mistakes."

"**I** am not worthy."

"**I** try to be a good person."

"**I** feel so unworthy."

"**I** lack Christlike qualities."

"**I** keep making mistakes."

"**I** haven't done enough."

"I could always do better."

"I'm not doing everything I should be."

"I have anger issues."

"I am not good enough."

When our focus is on "I," we will always fall short. Instead of asking, "Am I good enough?" we need to be asking, "Is Christ good enough, and am I in a relationship with Him?" We will never be good enough on our own, "for all have sinned and fall short of the glory of God,"[34] but Christ is good enough. If we are in a covenant relationship with Christ, we are good enough because Christ is perfect. Focusing on ourselves leads to disappointment, sadness, and anxiety, but if we put our trust in Christ and His perfection, we will be encompassed with a "lively hope"[35] and an assurance that we are perfect in Christ.

When we find ourselves repeating any of these "I" focused statements, we need to remember to replace our "I" with Christ's name. Christ is worthy. Christ is perfect. Christ is good enough. If we put our faith and trust in Him, we can declare with confidence the "I" statement, "I am perfect in Christ."

In summary, to determine if we are going to the celestial kingdom, we must ask, "Am I justified through Christ?" and not "Am I good enough?" We are saved by Christ's merits, mercy, and grace through justification. To be justified requires that we enter a covenant relationship with Christ through baptism, desire to do what is right, and then try to do what is right. When you are perfect in Christ, you can answer "yes" with confidence to the question, "If you were to die today, at the resurrection would you go to the celestial kingdom?"

Perfect in Christ

During my first-grade school year, my family moved from Provo, Utah, to Rigby, Idaho. Wasatch Elementary was just beginning its first year of Chinese immersion, and I was lucky enough to be part of it for six months before our move. Rigby didn't have a Chinese program, so, unfortunately, my Chinese instruction stopped. Even though I have never learned to speak Chinese, I have maintained an interest in China and its languages. One of the words I find intriguing in the Chinese language is the word *righteous* (Yì). This word is comprised of two components: a symbol for lamb (yángròu) on top of another symbol that means me (wǒ).

The Lamb Over Me = Righteousness

The Lamb of God makes us righteous. Just as this symbol suggests, when we enter a covenant with Christ, He covers us with His righteousness. Righteousness doesn't come by works but by a relationship with the Lamb. We should accept the invitation of the prophet Moroni to "Come unto Christ and be perfected in Him."[36] Righteousness comes from the Lamb, not the law.

Team Jesus

I love to play basketball and was really excited when I became an eighth grader and could try out for the middle school team. Even though I had been told that tryouts would be competitive, I wasn't prepared to see the seventy-plus kids who showed up with hopes of earning one of the ten to fifteen spots available on the team. To make the team, you had to be good enough. It didn't matter how hard you worked or how much you had improved since the previous year. It didn't even matter if you were a really good basketball player. To make the team, the coaches choosing the players had to decide you were one of the best basketball players. I was fortunate enough to make the basketball team that year, but I felt horrible for the other boys who had come to tryouts with me but didn't make the team. They came each day and worked hard, hoping at the end of the day they wouldn't be pulled aside by the coach and told, "Better luck next time. Keep practicing and maybe you will be good enough to make the team next year."

Salvation in the celestial kingdom is not like this at all. Christ doesn't merely take the ten to fifteen players who are good enough. He takes all seventy and gives them a Team Jesus jersey. The simple requirement to be on His team is a desire to play for Him. Everyone who desires to be on the team is accepted. We don't have to be a Stephen Curry or a Michael Jordan to make the team. In fact, we don't have to have any skills at all. On this team, we don't earn a spot. We simply have to accept Christ as our coach. We accept His offer to be on His team and put our trust in Him. All are allowed to play not because they deserve it but because of the love and grace of the team's amazing coach. When we, as players on Team Jesus, aren't performing well, our coach doesn't kick us off the team or make us sit the bench. Instead, our perfect coach allows us to keep playing and improving.

Joining Team Jesus happens in an instant. This is justification. When you join the team, it doesn't matter if your free throw shooting is 10 percent or 90 percent. You don't have to worry about being good enough. Whatever your percentage is, you are welcomed onto the team. Our coach, Jesus Christ, is a perfect free-throw shooter. He has never missed a shot. Our goal is to become a 100 percent free-throw shooter like He is. Once we are on His team, Jesus will help us improve our free throw shooting. He will guide us to become more like Him. This process of working to become a perfect free-throw shooter like Christ is the process of sanctification. We work to become a little better each week.

To become a better free-throw shooter, we can't just sit on the sidelines and do nothing. We actually have to go to practice, participate in conditioning and drills, and obey the coach. If we are truly interested in being on the team, we will go to the practices and follow the coach's directions. Christ has taught, "Ye shall know them by their fruits."[37] Our hours of practice show we are striving to follow the advice of Coach Jesus and we have a true desire to become like Him.

Although we will improve over time with practice, none of us will become a perfect free-throw shooter in this life. Christ knows it will take a very long time for us to become like Him. He knows we will continually make mistakes as we are learning. We will all miss shots and commit turnovers. Even the great NBA basketball player, Stephen Curry, misses more shots than he makes. Mistakes are a part of the sanctification process. They help us learn and grow. When we miss a shot, we repent, Christ forgives us, and we try again.

Some may mistakenly ask, "How good of a free throw percentage do I need to qualify for the celestial kingdom?" This is the wrong question. The question we need to ask is, "Am I on Team Jesus?" because everyone on Team Jesus is going to win. They are all going to go to the celestial kingdom.

Others may look at this analogy and think, "If we turn the ball over or miss a shot or score for the other team, Christ will say, 'You're off the team temporarily. Go repent, and then I will let you back on the team.'"

This is not the way Christ works. Jesus Christ is the perfect coach. He will never kick us off the team, even though we will repeatedly fall short. We are always free to leave Team Jesus, but Jesus will never kick us off the team. Christ has promised, "I will never leave you nor forsake you."[38] Jesus wants you on His team.

Why Troublest Thou the Master?

During Christ's ministry, a ruler of the synagogue, Jairus, came to Jesus and asked Him to heal his daughter, who was sick and going to die. While Christ was making His way to heal Jairus's daughter, a woman with an issue of blood for twelve years made her way through the crowd. Filled with faith, she thought, "If I may touch but his clothes, I shall be whole."[39] When she touched Jesus, her issue of blood was gone immediately.

While Jesus was speaking to the healed women, a man who had come from Jairus's house said to Jairus, "Thy daughter is dead: why troublest thou the Master any further?"[40] Jesus immediately said to Jairus, "Be not afraid, only believe."[41]

When we sin and make mistakes, Satan attempts to make us feel unworthy. Satan tries to convince us that it's all over and Jesus can do nothing for us. He will whisper into our ears, "You have sinned again. You are not good enough. Why troublest thou the Master any further?"

We may feel that we have fallen short too many times, but Elder Jeffrey R. Holland reminds us, "You have *not* traveled beyond the reach of divine love. It is not possible for you to sink lower than the infinite light of Christ's atonement shines."[42] No matter what you have done, Christ is there to forgive you and free you from your issue of sin. In response to your sins and mistakes, Christ says, "Be not afraid, only believe."[43]

The woman with an issue of blood could have given up. She had spent twelve years searching for a cure but to no avail. Instead of giving up hope, she reached out to the Savior and was healed. Jairus could also have given up since his daughter was reported dead. Instead, Jairus chose to believe in Christ.

Never give up hope. Believe in Christ. He is quick to forgive.

Conclusion

"Elder J. Devn Cornish taught in General Conference, "Our members often ask, 'Am I good enough as a person?' or 'Will I really make it to the celestial kingdom?' Of course, there is no such thing as 'being good enough.' None of us could ever 'earn' or 'deserve' our salvation... Let me be direct and clear. The answers to the questions 'Am I good enough?' and 'Will I make it?' are 'Yes! You are going to be good enough' and 'Yes, you are going to make it as long as you keep repenting and do not rationalize or rebel.' The God of heaven is not a heartless referee looking for any excuse to throw us out of the game. He is our perfectly loving Father, who yearns more than anything else to have all of His children come back home and live with Him as families forever. He truly gave His Only Begotten Son that we might not perish but have everlasting life! Please believe, and please take hope and comfort from this eternal truth. Our Heavenly Father intends for us to make it! That is His work and His glory."[44]

The individuals who responded in the survey that they are not going to the celestial kingdom because they are not good enough are technically correct. We are all sinners and therefore aren't "good enough." The Good News, however, is that even though we are not good enough, Jesus Christ is good enough. As we become one with Christ and put our faith and trust in Him, we become perfect in Christ. With Christ, we are good enough. We can declare with confidence, "I am good enough because of the great I AM."

Now that is Good News!

CHAPTER 4
THE GIFT OF JUSTIFICATION

"The Lord requireth the heart and a willing mind."

- Doctrine and Covenants 64:34

My dad took numerous classes from Dr. Stephen E. Robinson, the author of *Believing Christ*, while he was attending college at Brigham Young University from 1996 to 1999. He became friends with Dr. Robinson and spent many hours with him outside of class. During one of their discussions, my dad asked Dr. Robinson, "Did you think *Believing Christ* would sell so many books?" (*Believing Christ* was released in 1992 and became one of the bestselling LDS books of all time.)

Dr. Robinson replied, "I was sure hoping it would. Every semester I have hundreds of returned missionaries in my classes, and they don't understand the Good News of Jesus Christ. I knew the message of grace taught in *Believing Christ* was greatly needed by members of the Church. Even though the book has sold thousands and thousands of copies, my work is far from complete. Each semester my classes are still filled with students who don't know the Good News and who are trying to perfect themselves."

Dr. Robinson shared with my dad the words of a young Latter-day Saint missionary. In response to Dr. Robinson's declaration that you can't make yourself perfect, the missionary said, "Of course I can make myself perfect. That's the difference between Latter-day Saints and other Christians. They think they are saved by grace, that God hands them everything on a silver platter, and we know that we have to do it all ourselves, that we have to make ourselves perfect. I'm very good at what I do already, and I'm confident that I will have made myself perfect by the time I'm thirty or so."[45]

Twenty years later we still see this attitude among some Latter-day Saints. The following are some of the explanations we received from survey respondents:

"I am still working for it. By next year I should qualify."

"There is so much more I can do to perfect myself."

"I have a long way to travel."

"I haven't accomplished why I'm here yet."

"Because I need to prepare more."

"I try to better myself each week, but it doesn't mean I always get better."

"I don't know how obedient I've been, but I can also be very hard on myself."

"I still have work to do... things in myself to work on."

"I am not a perfect person."

"I'm still a work in progress."

These answers show that many members of The Church of Jesus Christ of Latter-day Saints feel they have to progress to a certain level of obedience before they qualify for the celestial kingdom. One of the individuals said, "I am still working for it. By next year I should qualify." What would happen if this person died tomorrow? Would this individual not go to the celestial kingdom because he or she hadn't progressed far enough toward perfection?

These individuals are confusing the process of sanctification with the instant gift of justification. Their statements refer to their journey on the path of sanctification as they progress toward becoming perfect like Christ. Their statements are correct. We do have a long way to travel. We do have to increase our obedience. We are a work in progress. The sanctification process begins in this life and continues into the next life.

The Good News is that once we are justified, perfect in Christ, we meet the requirement for the celestial kingdom—perfection. Once we are justified and made perfect in Christ, we begin the process of working to become like Christ. We don't have to achieve a certain level of progress toward becoming like Christ to be saved in the celestial kingdom. We are saved the moment we become perfect in Christ.

Parable of the Lifeguard

Imagine a lifeguard saying to a drowning woman, "I will save you once you improve your swimming ability." This would be ridiculous. Right? The lifeguard is not concerned about her swimming ability. The lifeguard just wants to save her from drowning. The woman doesn't have to be a good or perfect swimmer in order to be saved.

Likewise, the Savior doesn't say, "I will save you once you are more righteous or once you are perfect." He rescues us while we are drowning in sin. We humbly recognize we can't save ourselves, and we accept His rescue. Christ pulls us from the sea of sin, and we are saved.

Some resist being saved by the lifeguard. They are determined to save themselves. Any lifeguard will tell you that it is very difficult to save someone who is trying to save themselves. If you try, that person will just pull you down. You have to tread water until they finally give up, and then the rescue is easy. You just put a hand over their shoulder, and you swim back to shore. It's the same with our relationship with God.[46] God wants us to stop trying to save ourselves and trust Him to save us. We are not the lifeguard. We are the drowning swimmer.

Once Christ has safely brought us to shore, He will begin teaching us. Christ's goal is not to merely save us from sin but to also make us like Him—a perfect swimmer. The process of becoming a perfect swimmer takes a lot of practice and work. The practice and work to become a better swimmer doesn't save us from drowning. We have already been saved. If Christ didn't save us until we became a perfect or very good swimmer, we would all drown.

Will You Let Jesus Wash Your Feet?

During Christ's last meal with His disciples before His death, He tenderly washed and dried every disciple's feet. It's easy to miss the significance of this act in our world of paved roads, shoes, socks, and sitting down for a meal at a table with upright chairs where our feet are hidden. Circumstances were much different in Christ's time. People wore sandals and walked on the dirt roads of Israel to get from place to place. The disciples' feet would have been quite dirty. In addition to this, the people in Christ's day used low tables and lay on their sides as they ate, with their feet stretching out behind them. Although a person's feet were away from the table, their dirty feet would be evident during a meal, and so it was a normal practice for feet to be washed before a communal meal.

When Christ washed His disciples' feet, He was doing a job that was usually reserved for servants. This stunned His disciples. When

He offered to wash Peter's feet, Peter exclaimed, "Thou shalt never wash my feet."[47] To which Christ replied, "If I wash thee not, thou hast no part with me."[48]

Just as Christ offered to wash Peter's filthy feet, He has offered to wash away our sins. Like Peter, we may resist or reject His gift. Peter may have thought, "I can't let Jesus, the Son of God, wash my dirty, stinky feet. I should be washing His feet."

Like Peter, we may think we can't allow Jesus to wash our dirty, stinky sins. We aren't worthy to come to Him. Waiting for Jesus to cleanse us until we are worthy is like saying, "Let me wash my feet really thoroughly, and then I will let Jesus wash them." If we wait until we are worthy for Christ to cleanse us, we will be waiting forever since we have no power to cleanse ourselves of sin. If we reject Christ's offer to cleanse us until we are clean, we will hear the same rebuke Jesus gave to Peter, "If I wash thee not, thou hast no part with me."[49]

The only way to come to Christ is dirty. We must accept Christ's invitation to wash away our sins. Only He can make us clean.

Attempting to Be Saved by the Law

What does it mean to be justified? "To be justified is to be reconciled to God, pardoned from punishment for sin, and declared righteous and guiltless."[50] We each want to be justified, and we can achieve justification in two ways—through the law or by Christ. To be justified by the law, we have to keep all the laws all the time. We can't mess up even once because at the moment we commit a single sin, we become guilty and unclean and can no longer be justified or saved by the law. James taught, "For whosoever shall keep the whole law, and yet offend in one point, he is guilty of all."[51] There has been and only will be one person who keeps all the laws all the time and that person is Jesus Christ.

Hoping to be justified by the law is a path that only leads to discouragement and hopelessness because it's an impossible task. The apostle Paul says, "For no one will ever be made right with God by obeying the law."[52] Lehi echoes these words in the Book of Mormon saying, "By the law no flesh is justified; or, by the law men are cut off. Yea, by the temporal law they were cut off; and also, by the spiritual law they perish from that which is good, and become miserable forever."[53]

Since salvation and justification by the law is impossible, Lehi continues his teaching by declaring the only way to be saved. He writes, "Wherefore, redemption cometh in and through the Holy Messiah; for he is full of grace and truth. Behold, he offereth himself a sacrifice for sin, to answer the ends of the law, unto all those who have a broken heart and a contrite spirit; and unto none else can the ends of the law be answered. Wherefore, how great the importance to make these things known unto the inhabitants of the earth, that they may know that there is no flesh that can dwell in the presence of God, save it be through the merits, and mercy, and grace of the Holy Messiah, who layeth down his life according to the flesh, and taketh it again by the power of the Spirit, that he may bring to pass the resurrection of the dead, being the first that should rise. Wherefore, he is the firstfruits unto God, inasmuch as he shall make intercession for all the children of men; and they that believe in him shall be saved."[54]

Lehi testifies that all of those with a broken heart and a contrite spirit who believe in Christ will be saved in the celestial kingdom.

When you become one with Christ, He justifies you. Christ declares you righteous and guiltless even though you are far from perfect.

Are Works Required?

Are works required to be saved in the celestial kingdom? The Savior teaches, "Let your light so shine before men, that they may see your good works, and glorify your Father which is in heaven."[55] Christ has asked each of us to follow His example and go about doing good.[56]

Even though works are a crucial part of God's plan of happiness, it is vital we understand that works do not save us or earn us salvation. Works are required, but we must keep them in their proper place. Once we are justified and declared perfect in Christ, we begin the sanctification process to become perfect like Christ. What does it mean to be sanctified? To be sanctified means to be made holy. Works are a part of the sanctification process.

We can't become like God without any effort on our part. We can't simply say, "I want to be a heart surgeon" and then magically become one. We have to go to class, do our homework, and gain experience in the operating room. We have to develop the knowledge, skills, and attributes of a heart surgeon. The process of becoming like God is the same. It takes an inordinate amount of effort, but it's possible with Jesus Christ. Works assist us in becoming like God, but our works don't justify, save, or redeem us. Christ does the saving and redeeming.

Elder David A. Bednar teaches, "Our works and desires alone do not and cannot save us... we are made whole only through the mercy and grace available through the Savior's infinite and eternal atoning sacrifice."[57] Works cannot save us. Only the blood of the Lamb can make us whole. Works are a result of our faith and trust in the Savior, not a way to earn salvation.

Parable of the Two Debtors

In the New Testament, we learn of a Pharisee named Simon who wanted Christ to eat with him. Outwardly he appeared to be a righteous man, completing a list of obligations—keeping the commandments, going to synagogue, and praying often. When Christ was with Simon, a woman came and washed the Savior's feet with her tears and anointed Christ with oil. Simon wasn't pleased with this form of worship. Simon said within himself, "This man, if he were a prophet, would have known who and what manner of woman this is that toucheth him: for she is a sinner."[58]

Jesus perceived his thoughts and told him a parable, "There was a certain creditor which had two debtors: the one owed five hundred pence, and the other fifty. And when they had nothing to pay, he frankly forgave them both. Tell me therefore, which of them will love him most? Simon answered and said, I suppose that he, to whom he forgave most. And he said unto him, Thou hast rightly judged."[59]

Christ then taught Simon a powerful lesson, "Seest thou this woman?… I say unto thee, Her sins, which are many, are forgiven; for she loved much: but to whom little is forgiven, the same loveth little."[60]

Elder Dieter F. Uchtdorf taught in conference, "Are we like Simon? Are we confident and comfortable in our good deeds, trusting in our own righteousness? Are we perhaps a little impatient with those who are not living up to our standards? Are we on autopilot, going through the motions, attending our meetings, yawning through Gospel Doctrine class, and perhaps checking our cell phones during sacrament service? Or are we like this woman, who thought she was completely and hopelessly lost because of sin? Do we *love much?* Do we understand our indebtedness to Heavenly Father and plead with all our souls for the grace of God? When we kneel to pray, is it to replay the greatest hits of our own righteousness, or is it to confess our faults, plead for God's mercy, and shed tears of gratitude for the amazing plan of redemption."[61]

We are all sinners pleading at the feet of the Savior for mercy. We are all in need of His grace. We are indebted to Him. We must have confidence in the Savior and His righteousness, not our own good works.

Does Your Righteousness Exceed That of the Pharisees?

In the Sermon on the Mount, Jesus Christ declared, "For I say unto you, That except your righteousness shall exceed the righteousness of the scribes and Pharisees, ye shall in no case enter into the kingdom of heaven."[62] How can our righteousness exceed that of the Pharisees? After all, the Pharisees diligently followed the law and were "righteous." Unfortunately, the Pharisees sought salvation by keeping the law. In fact, they were so caught up in keeping the law that they didn't recognize Jesus Christ as their Savior, and in the end, they killed Him. The Pharisees didn't allow Christ to help them because they believed they were righteous and so they didn't need His help. Christ recognized this self-righteous attitude saying, "They that be whole need not a physician."[63] The Pharisees thought they were good enough and their works earned them salvation. They were going to be saved by the law.

How do we surpass the righteousness of the Pharisees? We become one with the "Son of Righteousness."[64] We humbly recognize and acknowledge that our righteousness comes through Christ—that we are "redeemed, because of the righteousness of [our] Redeemer."[65]

The Book of Mormon teaches us the attitude we should have. The prophet Alma declared, "Say: O Lord, forgive my unworthiness... yea, acknowledge your unworthiness before God at all times."[66]

Christ Is the Living Water

Would you rather drink from a natural spring or dig a well in hopes of finding water? For me, I would rather partake of the spring. Christ is our spring of living water. Many turn away from Christ's spring and try to dig a well on their own. They search tirelessly for water to quench their thirst. Jesus testified, "Whosoever drinketh of this water [well water] shall thirst again: But whosoever drinketh of the water that I shall give him [living water] shall never thirst; but the water that I shall give him shall be in him a well of water springing up into everlasting life."[67]

When you are in a covenant relationship with Christ, you can drink freely of Christ's living water. However, many seek another way to quench their thirst for salvation. Jeremiah 2:13 declares, "My people have done two evils: they have turned away from me, the spring of living water. And they have dug their own wells, which are broken wells that cannot hold water."[68]

Many unknowingly turn away from the Savior, the only source

of living water, and instead try to dig a well of works. When we try to quench our thirst by digging our own well of personal works, we will find our well will always be dry. This is because no matter how hard or how long we dig, living water cannot be acquired through our own efforts.

Christ teaches, "Blessed are they which do hunger and thirst after righteousness: for they shall be filled."[69] Nephi calls Christ the "Son of Righteousness."[70] When we thirst after righteousness, we are seeking Jesus Christ. We don't hunger and thirst after our righteous works; we hunger and thirst for He who is righteous. We must seek Christ, not our own works of righteousness. As we thirst after the Son of Righteousness, we will be filled with the living water of salvation.

Conclusion

Are you a work in progress? Absolutely. Do you have a long way to go? Of course. The question you need to ask is not "Have I traveled far enough on the path toward perfection to qualify for the celestial kingdom?" but "Am I on the path?"

Elder Bruce R. McConkie, an apostle of the Lord Jesus Christ, shared what is required to go to the celestial kingdom. He taught, "Everyone in the Church who is on the straight and narrow path, who is striving and struggling and desiring to do what is right, though is far from perfect in this life; if he passes out of this life while he's on the straight and narrow, he's going to go on to eternal reward in his Father's kingdom... If you are on that path when death comes because this is the time and the day appointed, this the probationary estate, you will never fall off from it; and for all practical purposes your calling and election is made sure."[71]

If you are on the path, you can say with confidence, "I am saved. I am going to the celestial kingdom."

Now that is Good News!

CHAPTER 5
PARTAKE OF HIS GRACE

"Ye shall have hope through the atonement of Christ and the power of his resurrection, to be raised until life eternal, and this because of your faith in him according to the promise."

- Moroni 7:41

Elder Shayne M. Bowen shared the following story in General Conference: "While serving as young missionaries in Chile, my companion and I met a family of seven in the branch. The mother attended [church] every week with her children. We assumed that they were longtime members of the Church. After several weeks we learned that they had not been baptized…

"Sister Ramirez advanced rapidly through the lessons. She was anxious to learn all the doctrine that we taught. One evening as we were discussing infant baptism, we taught that little children are innocent and have no need for baptism. We invited her to read in the book of Moroni: '…little children need no repentance, neither baptism… little children are alive in Christ, even from the foundation of the world; if not so, God is a partial God, and also a changeable God, and a respecter to persons; for how many little children have died without baptism!'

"After reading this scripture, Sister Ramirez began sobbing. My companion and I were confused. I asked, 'Sister Ramirez, have we said or done something that has offended you?'

"She said, 'Oh, no, Elder, you haven't done anything wrong. Six years ago I had a baby boy. He died before we could have him baptized. Our priest told us that because he had not been baptized, he would be in limbo for all eternity. For six years I have carried that pain and guilt. After reading this scripture, I know by the power of the Holy Ghost that it is true. I have felt a great weight taken off of me, and these are tears of joy.'"[72]

This woman was weighed down with guilt and pain for many years because she didn't know her baby boy was saved. Likewise, many members of The Church of Jesus Christ of Latter-day Saints don't know they have been saved. As a result, they have experienced years of unnecessary guilt and pain.

Our simple survey asked active Latter-day Saints, "If you were to die today, at the resurrection would you go to the celestial kingdom?" There were three possible answers they could circle: Yes, No, or I Don't Know.

Forty-eight percent of active Latter-day Saints answered, "I don't know." And in response to why they answered this way, many wrote, "I don't know," as their explanation. Other common explanations were that the criteria for the celestial kingdom were something we can't know. Here are the explanations that were given:

"I don't know."

"I will not know until that day."

"I guess I will find out when I die."

"Because I am not the judge."

"Only Christ knows the true criteria for such judgment."

"I am not the judge."

"Too sacred to talk about and personal."

"Christ is the judge, not me."

"I don't want to be prideful."

"Probably a 50/50 chance."

Alive in Christ

What if we were to ask these same individuals the following question: "If a seven-year-old were to die today, would he or she go to the celestial kingdom?"

I would hope one hundred percent of Latter-day Saints would answer yes to this question since it is clear that Christ has taught "all little children are alive in Christ."[73]

Elder Bruce R. McConkie, an apostle of the Lord Jesus Christ, wrote, "There is scarcely a doctrine so sweet, so soul satisfying, and so soul sanctifying, as the one which proclaims—*Little children shall be saved. They are alive in Christ and shall have eternal life. For them the family unit will continue, and the fullness of exaltation is theirs. No blessing shall be withheld. They shall rise in immortal glory, grow to full maturity, and live forever in the highest heaven of the celestial kingdom*—all through the merits and mercy and grace of the Holy Messiah."[74]

Joseph Smith's vision of the celestial kingdom contains this statement, "And I also beheld that all children who die before they arrive at the years of accountability are saved in the celestial kingdom of heaven."[75]

Are all children who die before the age of accountability automatically saved in the celestial kingdom? The answer is a thunderous and confident, "Yes!" There is no doubt or worry. There is no need to say, "I don't know," or "I hope so," or "I am not the judge," or "I will find out in the next life."

Is a seven-year-old living all the laws of the celestial kingdom? Is a seven-year-old perfect like Christ? Is a seven-year-old saved by his or her good works? Of course not. They are saved in the celestial kingdom "through the merits and mercy and grace of the Holy Messiah."[76]

Christ doesn't save most of these children or almost all of them. Christ saves 100 percent of children into the highest heaven of the celestial kingdom. When a child dies before the age of eight years old, we can be confident this child will receive the gift of exaltation.

Now let's change the scenario and say a child is baptized at age eight but dies tragically at age nine. What is this child's fate? Do we now have to worry and wonder if this child is going to receive the gift of exaltation? Do we simply have to hope this child has progressed far enough or has been good enough?

Whether we die at seven years old or nine years old, we are saved "through the merits and mercy and grace of the Holy Messiah."[77] If a nine-year-old is in a covenant relationship with Christ, he or she is alive in Christ and will inherit the celestial kingdom.

Christ and a Coin Flip

One of the more intriguing explanations given by a survey respondent was, "I probably have a 50/50 chance." According to this individual, if we die before the age of eight, we are guaranteed exaltation, but if we die sometime after we are eight, we have a 50/50 chance of making it. Are we going to get to judgment day and watch Christ flip a coin? Does it make any sense that Christ will save 100 percent of children, but He will only save 50 percent of adults who are on His team? Along these same lines, does it make any sense that we can know with confidence the salvation status of children under the age of eight, but we have no idea whatsoever about our salvation status if we manage to live past the age of eight? Using this flawed logic, we would be better off if all of us died in our early childhood.

The scriptures repeatedly teach that Jesus is "mighty to save."[78] Jesus is not just good at saving people. He is perfect at saving people.

He is not merely going to save some or most of the individuals on His team. He will save all who are on His team. Jesus is a perfect Savior. He is mighty to save.

Why can we answer the question, "If a seven-year-old dies, at the resurrection would he or she go to the celestial kingdom?" with such confidence? Because we know the doctrine that children are alive in Christ, and Christ saves all who are alive in Him.

Can we answer with the same confidence for a nine-year-old or ninety-year-old? Absolutely. Because we know the doctrine that all who are on Christ's team are alive in Christ. They are justified by Christ and declared perfect in Christ. The seven-year-old, nine-year-old, and ninety-year-old are all saved into the celestial kingdom "through the merits and mercy and grace of the Holy Messiah."[79]

Is It Prideful?

One of the respondents to the survey said they didn't want to say they were going to the celestial kingdom because, "I don't want to be prideful." Is it prideful to say that a baby who dies is going to receive exaltation in the celestial kingdom? Of course not. Similarly, it is not prideful to say an adult is going to the celestial kingdom because an adult is saved in the same way a child is saved—"through the merits and mercy and grace of the Holy Messiah."[80]

The only way this question reflects pride is if we believe our good works, not Christ's merits, qualify us or earn us salvation. When Ammon was rejoicing in those who had come unto Christ, "his brother Aaron rebuked him, saying: Ammon, I fear that thy joy doth carry thee away unto boasting. But Ammon said unto him: I do not boast in my own strength, nor in my own wisdom; but behold, my joy is full, yea, my heart is brim with joy, and I will rejoice in my God. Yea, I know that I am nothing; as to my strength I am weak; therefore I will not boast of myself, but I will boast of my God, for in his strength I can do all things; yea, behold, many mighty miracles we have wrought in this land, for which we will praise his name forever... Yea, we have reason to praise him forever, for he is the Most High God, and has loosed our brethren from the chains of hell... Who can glory too much in the Lord? Yea, who can say too much of his great power, and of his mercy, and of his long-suffering towards the children of men? ... Now have we not reason to rejoice? Yea, I say unto you, there never were men that had so great reason to rejoice as we, since the world began; yea, and my joy is carried away, even unto boasting in my God; for he has all power, all wisdom, and all understanding; he comprehendeth all things, and he is a merciful Being, even unto salvation, to those who will repent and believe on his name. Now if this is boasting, even so will I boast; for this is my life and my light, my joy and my salvation, and my redemption from everlasting woe. Yea, blessed is the name of my God."[81]

We should praise, rejoice, and boast in the redeeming and saving gifts of the Lord. Once we understand that we are saved by "relying wholly upon the merits of him who is mighty to save,"[82] we are filled with gratitude and not pride. When we recognize that we are 100 percent dependent on Christ for salvation, we are filled with humility and give all honor and praise to the Lord because we understand we are saved by His merits, mercy, and grace.

Does Not Knowing Change the Doctrine?

Many people have had a child die without knowing the good news that their child is guaranteed exaltation. Some even mistakenly believe their child is going to hell because he or she was not baptized or hadn't accepted Jesus as their Savior before they passed away. These parents are filled with depression, sadness, worry, anxiety, guilt, and fear.

Children who die before the age of accountability are saved regardless of whether their parents know and understand this doctrine. Even though the child's salvation doesn't change, the experience for the parents and family members who are still living is significantly different than it could be. If parents knew their child was saved in the highest level of the celestial kingdom, even though they would be devastated at the passing of their child, they would still be filled with peace, hope, and confidence for their child's future in the eternities.

Our survey revealed that 48 percent of active Latter-day Saints don't know if they are going to the celestial kingdom. These individuals, like the parents who lost a child without an understanding of Christ's grace, may be plagued with unnecessary worry, doubt, and guilt.

Cruise Ship Analogy

Elder Dieter F. Uchtdorf shared the following story: "There once was a man whose lifelong dream was to board a cruise ship and sail the Mediterranean Sea. He dreamed of walking the streets of Rome, Athens, and Istanbul. He saved every penny until he had enough for his passage. Since money was tight, he brought an extra suitcase filled with cans of beans, boxes of crackers, and bags of powdered lemonade, and that is what he lived on every day. He would have loved to take part in the many activities offered on the ship—working out in the gym, playing miniature golf, and swimming in the pool. He envied those who went to movies, shows, and cultural presentations. And, oh, how he yearned for only a taste of the amazing food he saw on the ship—every meal appeared to be a feast! But the man wanted to spend so very little money that he didn't participate in any of these. He was able to see the cities he had longed to visit, but for the most part of the journey, he stayed in his cabin and ate only his humble food. On the last day of the cruise, a crew member asked him which of the farewell parties he would be attending. It was then that the man learned that not only the farewell party but almost everything on board the cruise ship—the food, the entertainment, all the activities—had been included in the price of his ticket. Too late the man realized that he had been living far beneath his privileges."[83]

Once we have entered into a covenant relationship with Christ, joining His team, we board Christ's cruise ship, the old ship Zion. When we are on the boat, we are saved. Our works don't earn us our passage onto Christ's boat. Christ's blood paid for our tickets. He suffered and died so we could board the boat. Our job is to have faith in Christ, the captain, who is sailing us toward our destination of celestial life.

The man in Elder Uchtdorf's story desired to take part in the games, food, and activities on the ship. Similarly, 100 percent of Latter-day Saints who took our survey responded that they wanted to go to the celestial kingdom. Forty-eight percent of those surveyed said they didn't know if they were going, though. These individuals are unaware of the good news that the gift of eternal life in the celestial kingdom is for all those who are on Christ's ship. Like the man on the cruise ship who didn't know the food and activities were included in his trip, these individuals are unaware that they are saved and going to the celestial kingdom.

We don't have to pay extra to partake of Christ's feasts. Christ provides an all-you-can-eat buffet and it's paid for in full. It is a gift. The man on the cruise ship thought he had to pay for everything. Remember this: Christ has already paid the price for each of us. There is no additional payment required. You can't earn Christ's grace. Elder M. Russell Ballard taught, "Remember that we cannot get there by jumping out of the boat and trying to swim there by ourselves."[84]

We don't have to attempt to swim to the celestial kingdom by ourselves or stay confined to our room of works, eating our cold beans and crackers, when we could be partaking in Christ's hope and assurance that we are saved. Satan will try to trick us into thinking we have to pay for Christ's gifts and earn our salvation. However, we can't pay for a gift. Like the man in Elder Uchtdorf's story, far too many Latter-day Saints mistakenly believe they have to pay for everything on Christ's cruise ship. They believe in Christ but don't open His gifts. Christ wants each of us to receive His gifts of forgiveness, grace, peace, hope, and salvation.

Christ declares, "For what doth it profit a man if a gift is bestowed upon him, and he receive not the gift? Behold, he rejoices not in that which is given unto him, neither rejoices in him who is the giver of the gift."[85]

Some feel we have to be perfect or nearly perfect to get on board the old ship Zion. Elder M. Russell Ballard stated, "Too many people think Church leaders and members should be perfect or nearly perfect. They forget that the Lord's grace is sufficient."[86] Christ has paid the price for our tickets, and we only need to trust in Christ and walk on board.

Satan will work to deceive us into thinking that every time we sin, Christ kicks us off the ship. If this were true, no one would be on the ship for we are all sinners. Christ invites us onto His ship when we are sinners. Those who join Him (covenant relationship) on the ship are given the gift of justification and declared perfect in Christ.

Once on Christ's ship, we begin the sanctification process, each week working to become more and more like the Savior. All who are passengers on Christ's boat are sinners at different points along the sanctification path, but every passenger will arrive at the destination of the celestial kingdom. Elder M. Russell Ballard declares, "Our ship's destination is the full blessings of the gospel, the kingdom of heaven, the celestial glory, and the presence of God."[87]

Conclusion

If we are with Christ on the old ship Zion, we can know with confidence that we will reach the destination of the celestial kingdom, for "no waters can swallow the ship where lies the Master of ocean and earth and skies."[88]

Now that is Good News!

CHAPTER 6

CHRIST DOESN'T GRADE ON A CURVE

"Where sin was powerful, God's gift of undeserved grace was even more powerful."

- Romans 5:20, Contemporary English Version

My dad shared a story with me from his time as a student at BYU. He had a chemistry class that was crazy hard. On his first test, he got a score of 63 percent. My dad had earned an academic scholarship and was extremely worried that a D on this test would result in him losing his scholarship.

In class, following the test, the teacher informed the class that the highest score on the test was 72 percent. The teacher shared that since 72 percent was the highest score, he would have 28 percentage points added to each test. So, the person with the highest score went from 72 percent on the test to 100 percent. My dad's test score went from 63 percent to 91 percent. The test he thought he got a D on turned out to be an A.

We often hear that mortality is a test and as a result, we mistakenly apply what we have experienced with tests in school to how we will be graded on the test of mortality. One of the survey takers who answered, "I don't know" to the question about going to the celestial kingdom gave this as his explanation, "Maybe if graded on a curve."

My guess is that the person who said they might be going to the celestial kingdom if graded on a curve was referring to the grading method of my dad's chemistry class. The survey taker knows his performance in mortality is far from perfect (maybe performing at a terrestrial level), but if he can get some percentage points added to his performance based on the way everyone around him is performing, maybe this will push his grade high enough to make the cut for the celestial kingdom.

Bell Curve Grading

Some falsely believe their performance during the test of mortality will be graded on a curve. Using the illustration of bell curve grading may provide insights into how some view our final judgment.

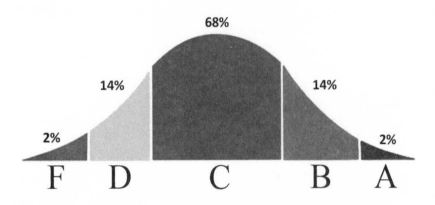

Pictured above is a diagram illustrating the breakdown of grades based on a bell curve. A teacher utilizing this grading system would only give the top two percent of the class A's. It doesn't matter how much time students put in or how hard they work. The only relevant factor is that a student performs better than ninety-eight percent of his or her classmates. Thus, the grade a student receives depends on how well he or she performs compared to the others in the class. Only the top performers will receive A's. Curves breed competition and comparison.

If we were to create a bell curve grading chart for the three degrees of glory, it may look something like this:

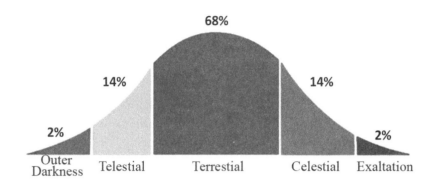

Christ doesn't grade on a bell curve. In the gospel of Jesus Christ, there is no competition or comparison with others. With a bell curve grading system, only the top few receive A's. With God's plan, every one of His children can receive the gift of exaltation in the celestial kingdom. Receiving the gift of eternal life comes from being in a covenant relationship with Christ, not as a judgment based on our performance compared to others.

While our time in mortality is sometimes called a test, Christ doesn't use a grading system to determine our salvation. Christ exalts all who are on His team. No one on the team is more likely to be exalted than another. Even though the team members have varying skill levels, all are still dependent on the merits of Christ for their salvation, and they all receive the same reward—exaltation in the celestial kingdom.

Some team members may do more than others, but everyone on the team receives the same reward. The player who makes repeated errors or has the lowest shooting percentage receives the same reward as the superstar on the team who scores all the points because both are on Christ's team and both are trying to do what Jesus asks of them. Also, whether you are on the Lord's team for one month or forty years, your gift is the same—exaltation in the celestial kingdom.

Jesus taught this principle in the parable of the laborers in the vineyard. "For the kingdom of heaven is like unto a man that is an householder, which went out early in the morning to hire labourers into his vineyard. And when he had agreed with the labourers for a penny a day, he sent them into his vineyard. And he went out about the third hour, and saw others standing idle in the marketplace, And said unto them; Go ye also into the vineyard, and whatsoever is right I will give you. And they went their way. Again he went out about the sixth and ninth hour, and did likewise. And about the eleventh hour he went out, and found others standing idle, and saith unto them, Why stand ye here all the day idle? They say unto him, Because no man hath hired us. He saith unto them, Go ye also into the vineyard; and whatsoever is right, that shall ye receive. So when even was come, the lord of the vineyard saith unto his steward, Call the labourers, and give them their hire, beginning from the last unto the first. And when they came that were hired about the eleventh hour, they received every man a penny. But when the first came, they supposed that they should have received more; and they likewise received every man a penny. And when they had received it, they murmured against the goodman of the house, Saying, These last have wrought but one hour, and thou hast made them equal unto us, which have borne the burden and heat of the day. But he answered one of them, and said, Friend, I do thee no wrong: didst not thou agree with me for a penny? Take that thine is, and go thy way: I will give unto this last, even as unto thee. Is it not lawful for me to do what I will with mine own? Is thine eye evil, because I am good?"[89]

Some people may think, "I am Mister Good Works. I have been a bishop and a stake president, I have participated in millions of service projects, and I have donated large sums of money to the church and other worthy causes. Surely I will receive a reward greater than the average Joe church member."

This line of reasoning reflects a grading by the curve mentality. Will Mister Good Works receive a greater reward than average Joe? Absolutely not! Since Christ doesn't grade on a curve, as long as average Joe has kept his baptismal covenant (is on Christ's team), he will receive exaltation, the same reward Mister Good Works will receive.

In fact, Mister Good Works' good works aren't what qualify him for eternal life. He is still a sinner and therefore if he were to be judged solely on his own merits, he would go to hell. His good works don't earn him a spot on Christ's team. Instead, Mr. Good Works does good works because he is on Christ's team. Some people mistakenly believe if they can complete enough good works during their lifetime, they will earn the reward of eternal life. We can't earn the celestial kingdom. Exaltation is a gift received from Christ, not a reward that is earned. Elder Jeffery R. Holland taught, "Our only hope for true perfection is in receiving it as a gift from heaven—we can't 'earn' it."[90]

Elder Dieter F. Uchtdorf proclaimed, "It is by God's amazing grace that His children can overcome the undercurrents and quicksands of the deceiver, rise above sin, and 'be perfect[ed] in

Christ.'"[91] You don't have to earn your salvation. You don't deserve salvation. Christ's amazing grace is sufficient.

Even though all will receive the same gift of exaltation, some will receive it faster than others. "If a person gains more knowledge and intelligence in this life through his diligence and obedience than another, he will have so much the advantage in the world to come."[92] What will be the advantage he has in the world to come? He will be nearer to becoming perfect like Christ because he is closer to living the principles of exaltation. Although he will not receive a greater reward than others, he may receive exaltation sooner by his diligence and obedience.

Conclusion

Some falsely believe that only the top few will receive exaltation, but the scriptures teach us otherwise. The chapter heading to Revelation chapter seven states that John sees the hosts of the exalted from all nations. Verses nine and ten read, "I beheld, and, lo, a great multitude, which no man could number, of all nations, and kindreds, and people, and tongues, stood before the throne, and before the Lamb, clothed with white robes, and palms in their hands; They called out in a loud voice: 'Salvation comes from our God, who sits on the throne, and from the Lamb!'"[93]

This scripture should fill us with a lively hope. The number of individuals who will receive the gift of exaltation is so enormous that no man can count them. Christ is not going to only exalt the top few. He is going to exalt all who are on His team.

Now that is Good News!

CHAPTER 7

I WILL GIVE YOU REST

"I am with you to bless you and deliver you forever."[94]

- Jesus Christ

I have learned that one of the ways the Lord speaks to us is through dreams. When I have a question, I ask the Lord for guidance through a dream. This is one of the dreams I had while working on this book.

In my dream, my dad and I were seeking shelter from a storm in Antarctica. We searched everywhere, but we couldn't find refuge. As we continued to follow a road, we discovered an enormous house. A kind Eskimo man lived there, and when he opened the door, he beckoned us to come in. Once inside, we were taken to a room filled with children.

Each child had a tiny Hot Wheels car in one hand and a large unopened Arizona energy drink in the other. The kids were racing their Hot Wheels cars around a table. The children were sweating as they worked hard to continuously circle their cars around the track. As the kids completed their endless loops, a wolf jumped through a nearby window. Shattered glass was propelled throughout the room as the wolf tried to find a victim to pull out into the cold. Before the wolf could do any damage, the Eskimo came and grabbed the wolf and hurled him out the window. While this commotion ensued, the children continued to run around the table, diligently working, but completely oblivious to the danger they had been saved from.

I prayed for the meaning of this dream and received the following interpretation: Christ beckons all to come into His house and to be saved from the storms of sin. When we enter into the house, we are justified and sheltered from the storm. As long as we remain in the house, the Eskimo (Christ), protects us.

Unfortunately, some individuals have made it safely into the protective care of Christ's house but are oblivious to the fact that He has already saved them. These individuals are represented by the children stuck sprinting around a table, clinging tightly to their energy drinks and miniature cars while endlessly running in a loop. The energy drinks represent the philosophies of the world, which may seem effective but are of no real benefit to us, while the Hot Wheels cars represent life when we try to do it on our own. When we seek to be the driver of our own lives, it is equivalent to being confined to a small table with a Hot Wheels car. We may work up a sweat with all of our efforts. We consume energy drinks for strength to keep going. We seek to rely on the arm of flesh and the ways of the world to achieve the strength to continue the relentless pace. Those at the table worked really, really hard but they were stuck in a loop—making no progress.

Christ wants all of us to progress, learn, and grow, but we can't do that at the confined table of works—trying to get somewhere by our own power and effort. We may feel we are progressing, but we are merely running in circles. To break free from this exhausting, endless loop, we must drop our energy drinks and Hot Wheels cars. We must realize we are not the power that is to drive the car. We must stop trying to be the driver and submit to the will and desires of Christ. We must break free from the table of works, enter the car driven by the Savior, and ride with Him to eternal life in the celestial kingdom.

Some believe working really hard is required to go to the celestial kingdom. In answer to the question, "If you were to die today, at the resurrection would you go to the celestial kingdom?" some people answered, "Yes" because they are trying hard. Here is a list of their explanations:

"Because I try hard."

"Because I'm trying as hard as I can."

"I am really trying."

"I'm trying hard."

How Are We Saved?

Prophets since the beginning of time have told us to look to Jesus, the Son of God, for our salvation. Christ came to redeem all mankind from their lost and fallen state. "For as in Adam all die even so in Christ shall be made alive."[95]

How are we saved from physical death? We are saved from physical death by the grace of the Lord Jesus Christ. How hard do we have to try to resurrect ourselves? Obviously, we all know this question is ludicrous. We receive the gift of resurrection because we chose to be on Christ's team in the pre-existence; therefore, we know that because we chose Christ, we will be resurrected by Him. We can't do anything to resurrect ourselves, no matter how hard we try.

How are we saved from spiritual death? To be saved from spiritual death, we must be perfect. Can we make ourselves perfect? Of course not. No matter how hard we try, we can never make ourselves perfect.

How do we receive the gift of eternal life in the celestial kingdom? We must be perfect in Christ. If we choose Christ in mortality, He will give us the gift of exaltation. We are saved by grace. By His grace, we are justified (declared holy) and sanctified (made holy).

Elder D. Todd Christofferson explained it this way, "One must choose Christ to receive what Christ offers… It is not that we earn these gifts, but rather that we choose to seek and accept justification and sanctification."[96]

Look to Christ and Live

"By small and simple things are great things brought to pass."

Alma 37:6

The Bible provides us a powerful type of Christ in the book of Numbers. "And the LORD sent fiery serpents among the people, and they bit the people; and much people of Israel died. Therefore the people came to Moses, and said, We have sinned, for we have spoken against the LORD, and against thee; pray unto the LORD, that he take away the serpents from us. And Moses prayed for the people. And the LORD said unto Moses, make thee a fiery serpent, and set it upon a pole: and it shall come to pass, that every one that is bitten, when he looketh upon it, shall live. And Moses made a serpent of brass, and put it upon a pole, and it came to pass, that if a serpent had bitten any man, when he beheld the serpent of brass, he lived."[97]

The Book of Mormon gives insight into this incident saying, "The Lord… prepared a way that they might be healed; and the labor which they had to perform was to look; and because of the simpleness of the way, or the easiness of it, there were many who perished… Now the reason they would not look is because they did not believe that it would heal them."[98]

The Lord's guidance was not complicated. It was simple and

easy. All who looked at the brass serpent were healed. The simplicity and ease of the invitation troubled many people. They expected a more complicated cure; a more elaborate treatment. They wanted to take action.[99] Sadly, many died because they didn't look. Since it was too simple, too easy, they failed to look to the serpent of brass and died.

The New Testament references this story saying, "And as Moses lifted up the serpent in the wilderness, even so must the Son of man be lifted up: That whosoever believeth in him should not perish, but have eternal life. For God so loved the world, that he gave his only begotten Son, that whosoever believeth in him should not perish, but have everlasting life. For God sent not his Son into the world to condemn the world; but that the world through him might be saved."[100]

Sadly, many today fail to follow the simple and easy invitation to believe in Christ and be saved. Although they are busy trying really hard to be good, they fail to believe in Christ and receive His grace. They fail to look to Christ and perish. Many have a hard time accepting the doctrines of grace, mercy, and justification by faith because they are "too simple," or "too easy."

Alma's advice to his son Helaman is instructive for each of us, "It is… easy to give heed to the word of Christ, which will point to you a straight course to eternal bliss… O my son, do not let us be slothful because of the easiness of the way; for so was it with our fathers; for so was it prepared for them, that if they would look they might live; even so it is with us. The way is prepared, and if we will look we may live forever… Yea, see that ye look to God and live."[101]

The Yoke of Christ vs. The Pillory of Works

When we enter a covenant relationship with Christ through baptism, we are yoked to Him. A yoke is a wooden beam fastened over the necks of two animals that enables them to pull a load together.

Christ taught, "Come unto me, all ye that labour and are heavy laden, and I will give you rest. Take my yoke upon you, and learn of me; for I am meek and lowly in heart: and ye shall find rest unto your souls. For my yoke is easy, and my burden is light."[102]

Satan has a counterfeit for the yoke of Christ. It's called the pillory of works. A pillory is a wooden framework with holes for the head and hands, in which an offender is imprisoned and exposed to public abuse. Striving to be justified and saved by our works puts us into a pillory.

If we can't describe our relationship with the Savior as being restful, easy, and light, we haven't yet received all the gifts of His grace. Are we yoked to the Savior, or are we trying to carry the load alone? Have we received Christ's gift of forgiveness or are we still trying to pay for our sins? Are we perfect in Christ or are we trying to perfect ourselves?

Some read these words of Christ and say, "Anyone who says it's easy doesn't know what they are talking about." These people are most likely in the pillory of works and haven't experienced the yoke of rest yet.

Too often, instead of bringing people to Christ's feet to find rest, we place them in the pillory of works by telling them to try the best they can to become worthy. Satan's counterfeit phrase to people in the pillory is, "I never said it would be easy. I only said it would be worth it." We might feel like this phrase is giving hope, but really, this saying just provides encouragement to endure the pain of the pillory.

Pillory of Works   Yoke of Christ

"Heavy load around your neck."
Acts 15:10-11, NCV

"My yoke is easy and my burden is light."
Matthew 11:30, KJV

Although the pillory and the yoke look similar, they are remarkably different. A pillory is a tool of torture and punishment. The yoke, on the other hand, is a tool of progress and unity. With the yoke, we are bound with Christ, moving forward together. In the pillory, we are stuck in one spot by ourselves. Our goal should not be to help people endure the torture of the pillory but to instead unite them with Christ, the Lord of Rest.

Two people can perform identical actions and one will be exhausted and worn out while the other will be renewed and strengthened. When we believe we must work as hard as we can to save ourselves, activities like going to church, reading our scriptures, keeping the commandments, and serving others all become burdens that deplete and exhaust us. Too many of us are filled with guilt and shame because we are not perfect, and we work tirelessly to earn Christ's forgiveness and salvation. We feel we must work hard to be declared worthy in His sight. This kind of life is not a life of enjoyment. This is a life of pain, torture, and depression that must be endured.

On the other hand, when we understand the truth that we are saved by Christ's grace, activities like going to church, reading the scriptures, keeping the commandments, and serving become a joy. These actions become rewarding to us and are a source of renewal and strength. When we know we are perfect in Christ, we are filled with hope, love, and peace. We rejoice in our salvation and eagerly go about with the Savior doing good. Psalm 84:5 states that there is "joy for those whose strength comes from the LORD."[103]

If we rely on our works and our own strength, we will fail. While our strength is finite and limited, God's strength is infinite and unlimited. We eventually run out of energy, but God never tires. It is time to stop trying to save yourself. It is time to let the Lord carry your burdens. It is time to surrender to Christ. It is time to partake of His rest.

Sacrifice Dream

On another occasion, I had a dream that also involved my dad. In this dream, my father told me the earth was so wicked that another sacrifice needed to be made to save humanity from its depraved and sinful state, and that I was to be this sacrifice. I knew what my father was trying to get me to do was wrong, so I ran away. For much of the remainder of my dream, I went from house to house, seeking refuge with various neighbors and friends throughout the United States. It seemed that no matter where I hid, though, my dad somehow found me and would try to sacrifice me.

Toward the end of my dream, I finally stopped resisting and consented to my father's request. As I was carrying an axe and a wood stump to be used for my sacrifice, a man appeared and walked alongside me. As we walked, the man gently said to me, "You don't have to be sacrificed to save mankind, Mitchell. I already did that." The man took both the axe and the stump from me and my dream ended.

In my dream, my dad represents things that testify of the truths we respect in our lives. Satan is good at twisting the truth. We know the scriptures are true, but Satan also uses the scriptures to teach his doctrines. He will twist the interpretations of scripture so a doctrine of Christ becomes a doctrine of the devil. Satan will use the scriptures to deceive us. He will twist truths in the scriptures to try and get us to work to save ourselves or work to pay for our sins. These twisted false interpretations of the scriptures may even come from a faithful and well-intending church teacher or leader.

In my dream, Jesus Christ came and took the tools away from me that were going to be used for my sacrifice. He taught me that since He had already come and suffered for mankind, I didn't need to pay for my sins or the sins of others. He had already paid that debt. Hebrews 10:18 tells us, "When sins have been forgiven, there is no need to offer any more sacrifices."[104] What was required of me was to put my faith in Him and strive to become like Him.

The scriptures teach us that Satan "seeketh that all men might be miserable like unto himself."[105] When we put our faith in our works, we will always feel like we are not good enough. This is because working harder will never make us good enough. The only way to become good enough is to receive the gift of justification and become perfect in Christ.

Bank Debt Parable

Let's pretend for a moment a man has a debt of $3 billion with a local bank. Although he has made payments for years, his payments don't even cover the interest that is accruing each month on the amount. One day, when he arrives at the bank to make a payment, he is told by the teller, "No payment is necessary, sir. An individual came in this morning and paid your debt in full."

Stunned, the man exclaims, "All of it?"

"Yes. All of it," the teller replies, smiling and nodding her head.

The man, completely overwhelmed by this stranger's generosity, desperately wants to know who this person is so he can pay this person back in some way. However, no one at the bank knows this good Samaritan's identity.

He is grateful and relieved that this massive debt is no longer hanging over his head, and yet joy and peace still elude him. That night he sleeps restlessly.

"It's not fair," the man thinks.

"It's simply not fair that this stranger paid off my massive debt and I'm not required to do something for this person in return. I have to do something."

He returns to the bank and finds the teller who assisted him the previous day. As the man arrives at the counter, he hands the teller a stack of cash.

"I am so grateful for the generosity and gift of the man who paid off my debt," the man begins, "but I must pay what I can. Here is a payment toward the debt."

Perplexed, the teller answers, "I can't accept your payment, sir."

"Take my money," he replies in a frustrated tone. "I must pay all that I can."

"All you can pay is $0," the teller insists. "There is no way for me to accept a payment because there is no longer a debt to make a payment toward. This account has been paid in full and is now closed."

"That can't be right," he pleads. "I have my money right here. Please take it."

"I'm sorry," the teller says gently. "You can't pay a debt that doesn't exist. Just accept your gift."

Like the man in this story, some of us are working tirelessly to pay a debt that doesn't exist. Christ has already paid the price for all of our sins. The debt has been paid in full. There is no way for us to pay for our sins because they have already been paid for. Our choice is to either receive this generous gift of forgiveness with gratitude and praise or reject the gift by attempting to pay the debt ourselves.

When we resist Christ's grace, we forfeit the peace and joy that come from accepting His gifts. In this story, the debtor foolishly believes he is showing gratitude by his efforts to pay off a nonexistent debt. We don't show gratitude by attempting to pay a debt that has already been paid. We show gratitude when we thank and praise God for His grace. We show gratitude by sharing the Good News that Christ has paid our debt of sin in full. We show gratitude when we receive Christ's gifts.

Walmart Analogy

Imagine a woman going to Walmart and filling her cart with items. When the cashier gives her the total, the woman says, "Well, for starters, I read my scriptures every day. I also shoveled my neighbor's driveway yesterday, and just this afternoon, I helped an old lady cross the street."

Confused, the cashier replies, "That's nice, lady, but how are you going to pay for these items?"

The woman replies, "I'm using my good works to pay for them."

"Sorry, lady," the cashier responds. "We don't accept that form of payment here. Wrong currency."

Elder Dieter F. Uchtdorf taught in General Conference, "Salvation cannot be bought with the currency of obedience; it is purchased by the blood of the Son of God."[106]

We cannot buy salvation or items at Walmart with the currency of good works. Salvation is paid for by the blood of the Lamb. Works are the wrong currency for salvation. Salvation is received as a gift from the Savior. This is the only way.

Christ's Buffet

Imagine going to a buffet restaurant with some of your friends, and one of your friends generously pays for your meal. Would you try to pay your friend back? If your friend refused to accept your money for the meal, would you try to pay the cashier for your meal again? Would you have such a fervent desire to be responsible for paying for your own food that you would walk to the back of the restaurant and start cleaning the dishes? Would cleaning the dishes change the fact that your friend already paid the price for your dinner?

Our friend, Jesus Christ, has already paid the price for our meal. Even if we want to pay for our own meal, we can't because it has already been purchased. Even if we choose to metaphorically work in the back, scrubbing dishes in an attempt to feel like we have worked for our meal of salvation, the reality has not changed. Christ alone has paid for our meal. It is a gift. It is not necessary to pay Him back. We simply need to be grateful. The prophet Isaiah teaches, "Every one that thirsteth, come ye to the waters, and he that hath no money; come ye, buy, and eat; yea, come, buy wine and milk without money and without price."[107] We need to come to Jesus Christ, the living water and the bread of life, and drink and eat of His grace freely.

Isaiah 55:2 declares, "Wherefore do ye spend money for that which is not bread? and your labour for that which satisfieth not? hearken diligently unto me, and eat ye that which is good, and let your soul delight itself in fatness." In the footnote for this verse, we are told that "spend" means "waste." Trying to pay for the gift Christ has already paid for is a waste. Are we guilty of wasting our time trying to pay for His gifts?

It is time we stop trying to earn our salvation by paying for our sins. The gifts of forgiveness and salvation are given "without price."[108] "They cost us nothing!"[109] Our job is to partake of His feast of grace with a broken heart and a contrite spirit, acknowledging that Christ has paid for a meal we can't pay for.

Prison of Sin

One day, during our family scripture study, we were reading Matthew chapter 25. We went around the table, with each person taking a turn to read a verse. "For I was an hungered, and ye gave me meat: I was thirsty, and ye gave me drink: I was a stranger, and ye took me in."[110]

When we got to verse 36, it was my brother, Enoch's, turn to read. He began, "Naked, and ye clothed me: I was sick, and ye visited me."[111] He then surprised us all with his departure from the actual text saying, "I was in prison and you broke me out."

Although our family laughed and laughed at his new scripture, the reality was that his reading was, in fact, accurate. Christ does break us out of prison. Christ suffered, bled, and died to set us free from the prison of sin. Jesus has blown the prison door off its hinges. However, some remain trapped in a prison that doesn't have a door! They work day and night with a plastic spoon trying to penetrate the concrete walls and escape. While they work tirelessly to free themselves, they fail to notice the door is open. It is time to drop the plastic spoon of salvation by works, take hold of the Savior's hand, and walk free. "Christ sacrificed his life's blood to set us free."[112]

Conclusion

Elder Jeffery R. Holland taught, "Every one of us is a debtor, and the verdict was imprisonment for every one of us. And there we would have all remained were it not for the grace of a King who sets us free because He loves us."[113]

Jesus endured the cross that you may be saved. Look to Jesus and live. He is the author and finisher of your faith.[114] If you look to Christ, trusting in His grace, you will inherit eternal life. It's as simple as 2+2=4.

Now that is Good News!

CHAPTER 8

JESUS SAVES THE SINNER

"[God] saved us, not because of the righteous things we had done, but because of his mercy."

- Titus 3:5, New Living Translation

PERFECT IN CHRIST

Elder Dale G. Renlund shared the following story in General Conference. "Some years ago a wonderful young man named Curtis was called to serve a mission. He was the kind of missionary every mission president prays for. He was focused and worked hard. At one point he was assigned a missionary companion who was immature, socially awkward, and not particularly enthusiastic about getting the work done. One day, while they were riding their bicycles, Curtis looked back and saw that his companion had inexplicably gotten off his bike and was walking. Silently, Curtis expressed his frustration to God; what a chore it was to be saddled with a companion he had to drag around in order to accomplish anything. Moments later, Curtis had a profound impression, as if God were saying to him, 'You know, Curtis, compared to me, the two of you aren't all that different.'"[115]

This story illuminates a powerful truth. We are all sinners. No matter how far we have progressed toward becoming like Christ, we still have a long, long way to go. Maybe Curtis had progressed a little further on the path of becoming like Christ than his companion, but when we look at the distance both still have to travel in order to become like Christ, the difference between the two is indistinguishable.

Joseph Smith compared learning the principles of exaltation to a ladder. "When you climb up a ladder, you must begin at the bottom, and ascend step by step, until you arrive at the top; and so it is with the principles of the Gospel—you must begin with the first, and go on until you learn all the principles of exaltation. But it will be a great while after you have passed through the veil before you will have learned them. It is not all to be comprehended in this world; it will be a great work to learn our salvation and exaltation even beyond the grave."[116]

For illustrative purposes, let's pretend the sanctification ladder to exaltation has one million rungs. Let's say our missionary, Curtis, was on rung 125 and his companion was on rung 100. Compared to his companion, Curtis may have felt that this twenty-five-rung gap was substantial. Curtis shouldn't have been comparing himself to his companion, though. Curtis's goal is to become like Christ, and Christ is at the top of the one-million-rung ladder. If we were to stand atop this one-million-rung ladder and gaze toward the bottom, we wouldn't even be able to perceive the difference between rung 125 and rung 100. From the top, the proximity of these two rungs would seem identical.

Elder D. Todd Christofferson shared the following story in General Conference, "Not long ago, a friend recounted to me an experience he had while serving as a mission president. He had undergone a surgery that required several weeks of recuperation. During his recovery, he devoted time to searching the scriptures. One afternoon as he pondered on the Savior's words in the 27th chapter of 3 Nephi, he drifted off to sleep. He subsequently related:

'I fell into a dream in which I was given a vivid, panoramic view of my life. I was shown my sins, poor choices, the times... I had treated people with impatience, plus the omissions of good things I should have said or done... [A] comprehensive... [review of] my life was shown to me in just a few minutes, but it seemed much longer. I awoke, startled, and... instantly dropped to my knees beside the bed and began to pray, to plead for forgiveness, pouring out the feelings of my heart like I had never done previously.

'Prior to the dream, I didn't know that I [had] such great need to repent. My faults and weaknesses suddenly became so plainly clear to me that the gap between the person I was and the holiness and goodness of God seemed [like] millions of miles. In my prayer that late afternoon, I expressed my deepest gratitude to Heavenly Father and to the Savior with my whole heart for what They had done for me and for the relationships I treasured with my wife and children. While on my knees I also felt God's love and mercy that was so palpable, despite my feeling so unworthy… I can say I haven't been the same since that day… My heart changed.'"[117]

Let's now add the mission president to our sanctification ladder. Since the mission president would have several more decades of learning, experience, and character development compared to the aforementioned missionaries, let's say the mission president had progressed all the way to rung 300 on this ladder. Although the gap of 175 and 200 rungs between the mission president and these young missionaries may seem considerable, it really isn't. If the mission president focuses on the gap between him and the young missionaries, he may be tempted to think he is righteous.

As mentioned before, however, the gap between us and others is not the gap we need to focus on. The gap to focus on is between us and Christ—the gap between us and the top of the one-million-rung ladder. Once again, from the view atop the ladder, the mission president's position would still be indistinguishable to the positions of the younger missionaries.

Like the mission president in Elder Christofferson's story, every one of us must realize that the gap between the person we are and the holiness and goodness of God is incomprehensible. When compared to Christ, we aren't all that different. We are all sinners—dependent on the grace and goodness of Jesus Christ.

I Am Righteous

Our survey results revealed that some Latter-day Saints believe they are going to the celestial kingdom because they are righteous. The following are responses we have received from individuals with this belief:

"**I** try pretty hard to be righteous, but it always doesn't work out. But for today, **I've** been really good, and based on today, **I** would go."

"Because **I'm** living how **I'm** supposed to."

"**I** am a righteous dude."

"Because **I** am trying to do what **I** am supposed to."

"Because **I** am not watching the Super Bowl." (This survey was taken on Super Bowl Sunday!)

"**I** am awesome."

"**I** like to think that **I** have done all things necessary to be worthy."

"Because **I** am righteous."

As I have done in chapter 3, I have bolded the use of the word "I" in each of these explanations. "I" is found in every one of these statements, but there is not a single reference to Christ. In chapter 3, we discussed the individuals who determined they weren't going to the celestial kingdom because they have claimed, "I am NOT good enough." The group we are discussing in this chapter are also "I" focused, but they are on the opposite end of the spectrum. They believe they are going to the celestial kingdom because they claim, "I have been good enough."

This group could be categorized as modern-day Pharisees. The New Testament Pharisees made it clear that they were not sinners. They were righteous. They were obedient. Declaring that you are righteous because of your good works is very dangerous and can result in rejecting the Savior like the Pharisees did in the New Testament.

On multiple occasions, the Pharisees criticized Jesus for associating with sinners—a group they were adamant they were not a part of. In response to the Pharisee's question about why He ate with sinners, Jesus said, "They that be whole need not a physician, but they that are sick.[118] I didn't come to invite good people to be my followers. I came to invite sinners."[119]

Christ shared many parables with the Pharisees to help them see the truth that they were sinners. Let's look at a few of these parables to help us examine the Pharisee inside of every one of us that wants to say, "I am righteous," instead of acknowledging the truth that "I am a sinner."

Parable of the Lost Sheep

Three of Christ's most well-known parables are the parables of the Lost Sheep, the Lost Coin, and the Prodigal Son. A key to understanding these parables is to examine what occurred before these parables were given. Luke chapter 15 begins with a group of sinners coming to hear Jesus. As usual, the Pharisees were murmuring about Christ's social circle, saying, "This man receiveth sinners."[120]

Christ responded to the Pharisees by teaching them three parables. The first one is the parable of the lost sheep. "Suppose one of you has a hundred sheep and loses one of them. Doesn't he leave the ninety-nine in the open country and go after the lost sheep until he finds it? And when he finds it, he joyfully puts it on his shoulders and goes home. Then he calls his friends and neighbors together and says, 'Rejoice with me; I have found my lost sheep.' I tell you that in the same way there will be more rejoicing in heaven over one sinner who repents than over ninety-nine righteous persons who do not need to repent."[121]

Do you want to be a part of the ninety-nine or the one? Initially, we may think, "I want to be a part of the ninety-nine. They are the righteous." As we examine this parable more closely, though, we might want to reconsider which group we want to associate with. Christ describes the ninety-nine as, "righteous persons who don't need to repent." The ninety-nine think they are righteous. In other words, the ninety-nine represent the Pharisees. The Good Shepherd can't save sheep that don't need to be saved. Christ can only save those who recognize they are lost.

In the parable, the shepherd doesn't return the lost sheep to the ninety-nine. He puts the lost sheep on His shoulders and brings the precious cargo to His house and has a celebration. As each sheep recognizes his or her need to be rescued by the Good Shepherd, Christ places him or her on His shoulders. The Good Shepherd brings him or her to His house and holds a celebration with the other sinners at His home. Yes, Jesus receives sinners into His house. The "righteous" remain in the open country.

The Book of Mormon teaches us the posture we should have before God. The prophet Alma declares, "Say: O Lord, forgive my unworthiness... yea, acknowledge your unworthiness before God at all times."[122] Only when we realize we are sinners can Christ save us. We must leave the ninety-nine righteous sheep who don't need to repent, and instead, we must declare our unworthiness before God and let Him carry us on His shoulders to His house.

After we are brought into Christ's home, we must resist the satanic temptation to proclaim ourselves righteous. Even after we are rescued into Christ's home, we remain sinners in need of repentance and improvement. The Book of Mormon teaches us to acknowledge our unworthiness before God at all times.

President Russell M. Nelson taught in the April 2019 General Conference, "Does everyone need to repent? The answer is yes. Too many people consider repentance as punishment—something to be avoided except in the most serious circumstances. But this feeling of being penalized is engendered by Satan. He tries to block us from looking to Jesus Christ, who stands with open arms, hoping and willing to heal, forgive, cleanse, strengthen, purify, and sanctify us. The word for repentance in the Greek New Testament is *metanoeo*. The prefix *meta-* means 'change'... Nothing is more liberating, more ennobling, or more crucial to our individual progression than is a regular, daily focus on repentance. Repentance is not an event; it is a process... We all need to repent."[123] We are all sinners.

Parable of the Lost Coin

The second parable the Savior teaches the Pharisees is the parable of the lost coin. "What woman having ten pieces of silver, if she lose one piece, doth not light a candle, and sweep the house, and seek diligently till she find it? And when she hath found it, she calleth her friends and her neighbours together, saying, Rejoice with me; for I have found the piece which I had lost. Likewise, I say unto you, there is joy in the presence of the angels of God over one sinner that repenteth."[124]

Just as in the parable of the lost sheep, one item is lost. Christ isn't ministering to the masses. He isn't rescuing two, ten, or a hundred at a time. He is rescuing one. Christ saves His children one by one. The focus of these two parables is on the one lost sheep and the one lost coin. The Savior was attempting to help the Pharisees identify that they were lost and in need of His rescue. The Pharisees didn't have eyes to see or ears to hear, though.

The Prodigal Son

The third parable the Savior taught the Pharisees was about two brothers. The younger son asked his father for his inheritance. After he received his inheritance, the younger son left for a distant country and wasted his inheritance on riotous living. After he had spent all his money, a mighty famine plagued the land. In an attempt to survive, he took a job feeding pigs and longed to satisfy his hunger by eating the pig slop.

"When he came to his senses, he said, 'How many of my father's hired servants have food to spare, and here I am starving to death! I will set out and go back to my father and say to him: Father, I have sinned against heaven and against you. I am no longer worthy to be called your son; make me like one of your hired servants.' So he got up and went to his father. But while he was still a long way off, his father saw him and was filled with compassion for him; he ran to his son, threw his arms around him and kissed him.

"The son said to him, 'Father, I have sinned against heaven and against you. I am no longer worthy to be called your son.' But the father said to his servants, 'Quick! Bring the best robe and put it on him. Put a ring on his finger and sandals on his feet. Bring the fattened calf and kill it. Let's have a feast and celebrate. For this son of mine was dead and is alive again; he was lost and is found.' So they began to celebrate.

"Meanwhile, the older son was in the field. When he came near the house, he heard music and dancing. So he called one of the servants and asked him what was going on. 'Your brother has come,' he replied, 'and your father has killed the fattened calf because he has him back safe and sound.' The older brother became angry and refused to go in."[125]

The Pharisees had created two groups—the righteous and the sinners. They were surprised and angered that Christ spent His time with the latter group. In this parable, the younger son is symbolic of a sinner, the older son symbolizes a righteous Pharisee, and the Father represents Heavenly Father.

In the parable, when did the young man come to his senses? He came to his senses when he realized he was a sinner. He declared, "Father, I have sinned against heaven and against you. I am no longer worthy to be called your son."[126]

In the parable, the Father gave the younger son his best robe, jewelry, and sandals. He held a feast and celebration for him. The older son was angry because he felt he had earned these gifts and yet had not received them. Now his father was giving these gifts to his undeserving younger brother. The older son said to his father, "Many years I have served you, and I never disobeyed a commandment of yours, but you never gave me a goat, that I might celebrate with my friends."[127]

The older son represents the attitude of the Pharisees, who think in terms of law, merit, and reward. Like the Pharisees, the older son declares he is righteous, saying, "I never disobeyed a commandment of yours." Does this sound like someone who has a broken heart and a contrite spirit? Of course not.

Some members of Christ's latter-day church identify with the older son. They think they are righteous. They have served faithfully in the church for many years. They have paid their tithes. They have fasted each month and paid their fast offerings. They think they have earned Heavenly Father's blessings.

What did the younger son do to earn or deserve the gifts he received from his father? He clearly did nothing to earn or deserve the gifts he was given. The Father is full of grace and forgiveness. The Savior was trying to help the Pharisees see that Heavenly Father's gifts can't be earned. They are not rewards. They are gifts.

The son who came to his father with a broken heart and a contrite spirit was given many gifts, even though he was full of sin. The son who thought he was righteous, on the other hand, did not receive these gifts.

The Savior taught the Pharisees these three parables in an attempt to help them see they couldn't be rescued until they realized they were lost. They couldn't be saved until they realized they were sinners. Like the older "righteous" brother, who refused to go into the party for his "sinner" brother, the "righteous" Pharisees refused to join the group of sinners who followed and worshipped Jesus.

The apostle John wrote, "If we say that we have no sin, we deceive ourselves, and the truth is not in us. If we confess our sins, [Christ] is faithful and just to forgive us our sins... and the blood of Jesus Christ... cleanseth us from all sin."[128]

Jesus Christ is the truth. If we say we are righteous, the truth [Jesus Christ] is not in us. In the parable of the lost sheep, the shepherd was not with the righteous ninety-nine. He was with the lost sheep. Likewise, throughout His earthly ministry, Christ was with the sinner.

The Pharisee and the Publican

In Luke 18, we find another parable that Jesus taught to those who "trusted in themselves that they were righteous."[129]

"Two men went up into the temple to pray; the one a Pharisee, and the other a publican. The Pharisee stood and prayed thus with himself, God, I thank thee, that I am not as other men are, extortioners, unjust, adulterers, or even as this publican. I fast twice in the week, I give tithes of all that I possess. And the publican, standing afar off, would not lift up so much as his eyes unto heaven, but smote upon his breast, saying, God be merciful to me a sinner. I tell you, this man went down to his house justified rather than the other: for every one that exalteth himself shall be abased; and he that humbleth himself shall be exalted."[130]

The Savior is telling us we should be as the publican in this parable and declare, "God be merciful to me a sinner."

The apostle Paul modeled this attitude when he declared himself a sinner saying, "Christ Jesus came into the world to save sinners; of whom I am chief."[131] Paul didn't say he was a sinner who is now righteous. He declared, "I am a sinner," in the present tense, even as an apostle of the Lord Jesus Christ. Jesus Christ saves us while we are sinners.

Nephi recognized that he was a sinner. He wrote, "O wretched man that I am!... My soul grieveth because of mine iniquities... My heart groaneth because of my sins; nevertheless, I know in whom I have trusted."[132] Like the apostle Paul, Nephi didn't say, "I used to be a wretched man." He said, "I am a wretched man."

Nephi did not trust in himself or his righteousness. Nephi trusted in the Lord saying, "O Lord, I have trusted in thee, and I will trust in thee forever. I will not put my trust in the arm of flesh... O Lord, I will praise thee forever; yea, my soul will rejoice in thee, my God, and the rock of my salvation... May the gates of hell be shut continually before me, because that my heart is broken and my spirit is contrite! O Lord, wilt thou encircle me around in the robe of thy righteousness!"[133]

Conclusion

The prophet Nephi realized he was a wretched man. Paul recognized he was a sinner. If we lose "sight of our sinfulness, we lose sight of our need for the One who has come to heal the sinner."[134] Christ didn't come to save the righteous. He came to save the sinner. Now that is Good News!

CHAPTER 9

YOU ARE SAVED BY GRACE

"And he [Christ] said unto me [Paul], My grace is sufficient for thee: for my strength is made perfect in weakness. Most gladly therefore will I rather glory in my infirmities, that the power of Christ may rest upon me… for when I am weak, then am I strong."

- 2 Corinthians 12:9–10, King James Version

I am always trying to share the good news with those around me. It is very common when I share a thought in one of my church classes about being saved by grace for the teacher or a classmate to say, "Yes, but after all we can do," or "We must do all we can and then Christ makes up the difference." These comments bring great sadness to my heart.

These comments about grace are not unique to my church classes. Our survey showed that many Latter-day Saints believe they will go to the celestial kingdom because Christ will make up the difference. The following are explanations given from those surveyed that fit into this category:

"I am trying to do as God asked me, and I believe that God will provide the rest through and because of His atonement."

"Because I'm trying, and Christ makes up the rest."

"Because Christ makes up the difference."

After All We Can Do?

I believe the common misconception that we do all we can and then Christ makes up the difference has come from a misinterpretation of 2 Nephi 25:23, "For we labor diligently to write, to persuade our children, and also our brethren, to believe in Christ, and to be reconciled to God; for we know that it is by grace that we are saved, after all we can do."

Some have turned this powerful verse on the doctrine of grace into support for their belief in salvation by works. Dr. Stephen E. Robinson, the author of the book *Believing Christ*, wrote of this verse, "At first glance at this scripture, we might think that grace is offered to us only chronologically after we have completed doing all we can do, but this is demonstrably false, for we have already received many manifestations of God's grace before we even come to this point…

"Actually, I understand the preposition 'after' in 2 Nephi 25:23 to be a preposition of separation rather than a preposition of time. It denotes logical separateness rather than temporal sequence. We are saved by grace 'apart from all we can do,' or 'all we can do notwithstanding,' or even 'regardless of all we can do.' Another acceptable paraphrase of the sense of the verse might read, 'We are still saved by grace, after all is said and done.'

"In addition, even the phrase 'all we can do' is susceptible to a sinister interpretation as meaning every single good deed we could conceivably have ever done. This is nonsense. If grace could operate only in such cases, no one could ever be saved, not even the best among us. It is precisely because we don't always do everything we could have done that we need a Savior in the first place, so obviously we can't make doing everything we could have done a condition for receiving grace and being saved!

"Thus, the correct sense of 2 Nephi 25:23 would be that we are ultimately saved by grace apart from whatever we manage to do. Grace is not merely a decorative touch or a finishing bit of trim to top off our own efforts—it is God's participation in the process of our salvation from its beginning to its end."[135]

Elder Dieter F. Uchtdorf taught in General Conference, "I wonder if sometimes we misinterpret the phrase 'after all we can do.' We must understand that 'after' does not equal 'because.' We are not saved 'because' of all that we can do. Have any of us done *all* that we can do? Does God wait until we've expended every effort before He will intervene in our lives with His saving grace?"[136] The answer to these questions is an emphatic no. Christ doesn't make up the difference only after our best efforts. The Book of Mormon makes this very clear. 2 Nephi 10:24 reads, "It is only in and through the grace of God that ye are saved."

The Book of Mormon teaches the doctrine of grace beautifully but some interpret the book through their "perfect by performance" glasses. They turn the beautiful doctrine of grace into the satanic lie of salvation by works.

His Grace Is Sufficient

At the beginning of his talk entitled "His Grace is Sufficient," Brad Wilcox shares the following story:

A BYU student once came to me and asked if we could talk. I said, "Of course. How can I help you?"

She said, "I just don't get grace."

I responded, "What is it that you don't understand?"

She said, "I know I need to do my best and then Jesus does the rest, but I can't even do my best."

She then went on to tell me all the things she should be doing because she's a Mormon that she wasn't doing.

She continued, "I know that I have to do my part and then Jesus makes up the difference and fills the gap that stands between my part and perfection. But who fills the gap that stands between where I am now and my part?"

She then went on to tell me all the things that she shouldn't be doing because she's a Mormon, but she was doing them anyway.

Finally I said, "Jesus doesn't make up the difference. Jesus makes all the difference. Grace is not about filling gaps. It is about filling us."

Seeing that she was still confused, I took a piece of paper and drew two dots—one at the top representing God and one at the bottom representing us. I then said, "Go ahead. Draw the line. How much is our part? How much is Christ's part?"

She went right to the center of the page and began to draw a line. Then, considering what we had been speaking about, she went to the bottom of the page and drew a line just above the bottom dot.

I said, "Wrong."

She said, "I knew it was higher. I should have just drawn it because I knew it."

I said, "No. The truth is, there is no line. Jesus filled the whole space. He paid our debt in full. He didn't pay it all except for a few coins. He paid it all. It is finished."

She said, "Right! Like I don't have to do anything?"

"Oh no," I said, "you have plenty to do, but it is not to fill that gap."

What Role Do Our Works Play?

The doctrines of grace, justification, and sanctification do not remove or reduce the need for obedience. These doctrines simply put obedience in its proper place.

"Whenever the full extent of God's amazing grace is explained and applied, some react with alarm. They see it as a swing too far in the direction of God's mercy and love. They fear that if you say that works and obedience do not earn our salvation, then that gives us license to sin. That is not the case. Since the first century people have been twisting the doctrine of salvation by grace to indulge themselves, but that shouldn't be a reason to stop teaching the true doctrine of grace. False teachings about grace are dangerous but the true doctrine of salvation by grace does not lead to moral irresponsibility or lazy passivity or disobedience. Rather, it is a strong, vibrant, and holy truth that will lead to a successful and fulfilling life. True grace will never lead a man to more sin but rather to a fuller repentance. Understanding and believing the doctrine of salvation by grace is one of the most powerful life-changing doctrines. Although there is a tendency in people to twist the beautiful doctrine of grace into something ugly, the real danger is to ignore grace entirely."[137]

Are You Saved by Works?

On a hot day in Hawaii, my dad and his companion were tracting, looking for someone to teach the good news of Jesus Christ. After knocking on countless doors and being rejected, a woman answered the door. She recognized that they were missionaries for The Church of Jesus Christ of Latter-day Saints and asked, "Do you believe you are saved by works?" Before my dad could answer, his companion responded, "Yes, we are saved by works." The woman replied, "Then you are not representatives of the Lord Jesus Christ" and shut the door.

How are we saved? Are we saved by works or are we saved by the Lord Jesus Christ? If we do our part and then Christ makes up the difference, what portion of our resurrection are we responsible for? Are we to perform as much of the resurrection as we can and then Christ finishes what we can't? Of course not. Christ does 100 percent of the resurrection. Our rescue from spiritual death is the same process as our rescue from physical death. We do all we can, which is nothing, and Jesus does the rest—100 percent!

The apostle Paul continually had to teach the saints of his day that salvation is a gift from God, not a reward for good works. To correct those who were seeking to be saved by the law, Paul taught, "A man is not justified by the works of the law, but by the faith of Jesus Christ, even we have believed in Jesus Christ, that we might be justified by the faith of Christ, and not by the works of the law: for by the works of the law shall no flesh be justified… but Christ liveth in me: and the life which I now live in the flesh I live by the faith of the Son of God, who loved me, and gave himself for me. I do not frustrate the grace of God: for if righteousness come by the law, then Christ is dead in vain."[138]

Some misunderstand the statements that Christ does 100 percent of the saving to mean nothing is required on our part. This response is illustrated in the example shared by Brad Wilcox as he tried to teach the BYU student about grace, she said, "Right! Like I don't have to do anything?" Yes, there is work to do to become like Christ. Since works are required to become like Christ, some erroneously jump to the conclusion that our works do part of the saving. Works are required and essential, but they don't do the saving. Christ does 100 percent of the saving.

When we are asked, "Are you saved by works?" we should answer with confidence, "No, I am saved by the Lord Jesus Christ." The doctrine that we do our part and Christ makes up the difference is false.

My dad's missionary companion didn't understand the true doctrine of grace and as a result, he taught a false gospel of salvation by works. We are commanded by the Lord to teach our children the gospel. The word "gospel" is derived from a word meaning "good news" or "glad tidings." What is the good news we need to ensure we know and understand so we don't teach the false doctrine salvation by works like my dad's missionary companion?

Paul summarizes the good news succinctly in Romans 5:8. "While we were yet sinners, Christ died for us." Even though we will sin and miss the mark daily, we can be in a saved condition through the redeeming blood of Jesus Christ. Jesus doesn't wait for us to reach perfection to save us. He saves us while we are sinners. The good news is that we are called Saints not because we are righteous but because we are sinners who keep trying.

Forgiveness and salvation are not gifts to be received in the future. They are gifts the Lord wants us to receive in the present. Christ didn't say, "Your sins *will be* forgiven." Instead, he used the present tense, stating, "Your sins *are* forgiven."[139] There is power in declaring, "I am saved" in the present tense instead of "I will be saved" or "I hope to be saved."

When Christ came to the home of Zacchaeus, a short man who climbed a sycamore tree to see Jesus, He said, "This day is salvation come to this house... For the Son of man is come to seek and to save that which was lost."[140] Christ wants each of us to accept the gift of salvation today, not in the future or after we have expended our best efforts.

We want to be sure that every young man and woman have received Christ's gift of salvation so they can bring this gift to the homes of others. We want to make sure when our young men and women serve as full-time missionaries, they teach the good news of God's grace and not the false gospel of works.

Conclusion

A belief that we do our part and then Christ makes up the difference "is mockery before God, denying the mercies of Christ, and the power of his Holy Spirit, and putting trust in dead works."[141]

Mosiah 3:17 declares, "And moreover, I say unto you, that there shall be no other name given nor any other way nor means whereby salvation can come unto the children of men, only in and through the name of Christ, the Lord Omnipotent." There is no other name given. Not mine. Not yours. The only name by which we are saved is Jesus Christ. Jesus does 100 percent of the saving.

Now that is Good News!

CHAPTER 10

I WILL NEVER LEAVE YOU

"Let no man glory in man, but rather let him glory in God."

- Doctrine and Covenants 76:61

A speaker in one of our recent sacrament meetings, in an attempt to give the members of our congregation hope and confidence, said, "Some of you are wondering if you died today where would you go? I want you to know that if you are doing your best and you die, you will go to the celestial kingdom." Later that day, in another church meeting, one of our instructors was teaching about grace and said, "If you are doing your best, then you will receive God's grace."

These individuals were attempting to teach the Good News of Jesus Christ. They were trying to convey a message of hope to those listening. What they taught, however, was not the truth, but instead was a doctrine of the devil. These false doctrines are similar to the misinterpretation of the scripture, "It is by grace that we are saved, after all we can do."[142] These statements are incorrectly teaching that we are saved by grace, once we have done our personal best.

The belief that we are saved by doing our personal best was a common response to our survey. The following are some of the explanations:

"I'm doing my best."

"I'm doing my best to keep my covenants."

"I'm trying the best I can."

"Striving each day to do my best."

"I am trying to do my best."

"I am giving my best efforts."

"I am doing the best I can."

Hurdle Analogy

My cousin, Brooklyn, is on our high school track team and is an amazing hurdler. When she runs a race, she is not only racing against the other runners, but she is also racing against herself in an attempt to set a new personal record. Throughout the track season, Brooklyn often walks off the field with a blue ribbon since she beat all of the other racers, yet on many of these occasions, even though she beat the other racers, she didn't achieve her own personal best time.

In fact, Brooklyn may set a new personal record at a meet one weekend, but during her next race the following weekend, she may hit a hurdle, fall to the ground, and finish with her worst time ever. Like Brooklyn, we don't always do the best we are capable of, so if we only receive grace when we do our personal best, we will rarely receive grace since we are capable of doing better.

The truth is that the race of life is not a steady, uphill progression but instead is filled with daily peaks and valleys. Some days we are on top and other days, despite our desires and efforts, we fall short of the stellar performance we have achieved on previous days. If we have run the best race we have ever run, we can be confident and feel good that we will receive grace. But in the race when we hit a hurdle and fall down, we know this wasn't our best effort and thus we aren't going to receive Christ's grace. This is why the belief, "I'm saved if I'm doing my best," is so dangerous. We need Christ precisely when we hit hurdles and fall down in life. We need Him the most when we are at our worst. We don't just need Christ during our best races. We need Him in every race.

Is My Mom Doing Her Best?

My mom is a wonderful disciple of Christ, but at times she loses her patience and raises her voice. When my mom raises her voice in frustration, is she doing her best? No. How do I know this? I know this because many times in similar situations she doesn't raise her voice; therefore, when she raises her voice in frustration, she is not doing her best. When my mom isn't doing her best, is she unworthy of Christ's grace? Is my mom no longer in a saved condition when she isn't doing her best? Does my mom need to hope she dies on a day that she hasn't raised her voice if she wants to be saved? Of course not. My mom is a disciple of Christ both on the days she raises her voice and the days she doesn't. As a disciple of Christ, she is saved even though she sometimes doesn't do her best.

Christ Will Never Leave You

Many disciples of Christ are battling an addiction to pornography. The addict's personal best would be to never look at pornography. A recovering addict may go days, weeks, or years between relapses. When the addict relapses, does he lose Christ's grace because he has not done his best? Like the hurdler, the addict needs Christ's grace the most when he falls. If the addict must do his best in order to receive Christ's grace, he would be excluded from Christ's grace at the moment of his relapse, which is when he needs Christ's grace the most.

Christ doesn't say, "I am with you as long as you are doing your best," but He does say, "I am with you always… I will never leave you nor forsake you."[143]

Conclusion

Doing our best cannot be a condition for receiving Christ's grace or being saved in the celestial kingdom. If this were the case, none of us would receive grace or be saved. We need a Savior precisely because we don't always do our best. When we teach that we must do our personal best to receive grace and salvation, we are subtly changing the hopeful doctrine of grace into a doctrine of depression.

Try searching the scriptures to find references that teach, "We are saved when we do our best." You will not find even one. Why will you not find any? Because this teaching is a doctrine of the devil.

One of my favorite scriptures is found in Zephaniah 3:17, "The LORD your God is with you. He is a hero who saves you. He happily rejoices over you, renews you with his love, and celebrates over you with shouts of joy."[144]

Now that is Good News!

CHAPTER 11

REJOICE IN CHRIST

"Happy is he that hath the God of Jacob for his help, whose hope is in the LORD his God."

- Psalm 146:5, King James Version

I have been homeschooled most of my life. For the past ten years, I have been a part of a homeschool co-op where a bunch of homeschoolers meet to learn together. This co-op is held at Christ Community Church (CCC). The co-op is a mixture of Latter-day Saints and families that attend CCC. As I talk with my friends about Jesus, it has been interesting to see how my friends who attend CCC talk about Jesus and how my Latter-day-Saint friends talk about Jesus.

I have noticed these differences in common expressions. My friends from CCC say, "I am grateful for Jesus," while my Latter-day Saint friends say, "I am grateful for the atonement."

My friends from CCC say, "Jesus has saved me," while my Latter-day Saint friends say, "I can use the atonement."

My friends from CCC say, "I can do all things through Christ who strengthens me," while my Latter-day Saint friends say, "The enabling power of the atonement."

The way the word atonement is commonly used by Latter-day Saints didn't feel right to me so I began studying to see if I could determine why I felt this way. In my studies, I read a conference talk from President Russell M. Nelson that addresses this very issue. Our prophet has given us this counsel, "It is doctrinally incomplete to speak of the Lord's atoning sacrifice by shortcut phrases, such as 'the atonement' or 'the enabling power of the atonement' or 'applying the atonement' or 'being strengthened by the atonement.' These expressions present a real risk of misdirecting faith by treating the *event* as if *it* had living existence and capabilities independent of our Heavenly Father and His Son, Jesus Christ. Under the Father's great eternal plan, it is the Savior who suffered. It is the Savior who broke the bands of death. It is the Savior who paid the price for our sins and transgressions and blots them out on condition of our repentance. It is the Savior who delivers us from physical and spiritual death. There is no amorphous entity called 'the atonement' upon which we may call for succor, healing, forgiveness, or power. Jesus Christ is the source."[145]

President Nelson is teaching us that we don't give thanks, honor, and praise to an event. Instead, we give thanks, honor, and praise to a person—Jesus Christ, the Savior and Redeemer of the world. We should look to Christ, not the atonement, for a remission of our sins.

Mother's Day Analogy

Pretend for a moment you have been invited to speak in sacrament meeting on Mother's Day and you begin your message by saying something like this:

"January 27, 2003, is very special to me. It is the day I was born into the world. I am so grateful for my date of birth. I don't know where I would be without my birthday. If it weren't for my birthday, I would've been lost. I have received so much strength and comfort from my birthday. I have learned so much from my birthday. I love my birthday."

If you gave such a talk, it might bring tears to your mother's eyes, but not tears of happiness since you would be giving honor, praise, and thanks to the event of your birth instead of giving honor, praise, and thanks to your mother, the person who gave you life.

ARE YOU GIVING THANKS, PRAISE, AND HONOR TO THE EVENT OR TO THE CHRIST?

Calendar 33 AD

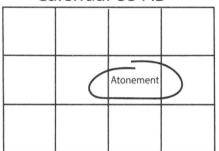

Jesus Christ

Calendar 33 AD	Jesus Christ
1. I'm grateful for the Atonement.	1. I'm grateful for my Savior, Jesus Christ.
2. The Atonement strengthens me.	2. Jesus Christ gives me strength.
3. I'm grateful that I can be forgiven through the Atonement.	3. I'm grateful for Jesus Christ's forgivness.
4. How do I apply the Atonement in my life?	4. How can I recieve Christ's grace?
5. The power of the Atonement.	5. The power of Jesus Christ.

Like our births, the atonement is an event. You should not put your faith and trust in an event but should instead put your faith and trust in the Redeemer. Christ bled from every pore. Christ forgives you. Christ comforts you. Christ heals you. Christ saves you. Give thanks to the source (Jesus Christ)—not an event (the atonement).

Conclusion

Based on the content of many of the talks and lessons given in our current church meetings, one would think 2 Nephi 25:26 reads, "We talk of the atonement, we rejoice in the atonement, and we preach of the atonement." It is time to stop rejoicing in the atonement and start rejoicing in Christ.

2 Nephi 25:26 reads, "And we talk of Christ, we rejoice in Christ, we preach of Christ, we prophesy of Christ, and we write according to our prophecies, that our children may know to what source they may look for a remission of their sins."

Now that is Good News!

CHAPTER 12

I WILL GIVE YOU A NEW HEART

"Christ is in you. He is your hope of glory."

- Colossians 1:27, New International Reader's Version

President David O. McKay had a vision of heaven in 1921 while visiting the islands of Samoa. While in vision, President McKay asked the Savior a question. He wanted to know who would inherit the celestial kingdom. President McKay recorded his vision, and the Savior's answer to his question was as follows:

"We sailed all day on the smoothest sea of our entire trip. Towards evening, the reflection of the afterglow of a beautiful sunset was most splendid! The sky was tinged with pink, and the clouds lingering around the horizon were fringed with various hues of crimson and orange, while the heavy cloud farther to the west was somber purple and black. These various colors cast varying shadows on the peaceful surface of the water. Those from the cloud were long and dark, those from the crimson-tinged sky, clear but rose-tinted and fading into a faint pink that merged into the clear blue of the ocean. Gradually, the shadows became deeper and heavier, and then all merged into a beautiful calm twilight that made the sea look like a great mirror upon which fell the faint light of the crescent moon!

"Pondering still upon this beautiful scene, I lay in my berth at ten o'clock that night, and thought to myself: Charming as it is, it doesn't stir my soul with emotion as do the innocent lives of children, and the sublime characters of loved ones and friends. Their beauty, unselfishness, and heroism are, after all, the most glorious!

"I then fell asleep, and beheld in vision something infinitely sublime. In the distance, I beheld a beautiful white city. Though far away, yet I seemed to realize that trees with luscious fruit, shrubbery with gorgeously-tinted leaves, and flowers in perfect bloom abounded everywhere. The clear sky above seemed to reflect these beautiful shades of color. I then saw a great concourse of people approaching the city. Each one wore a white flowing robe, and a white headdress. Instantly my attention seemed centered upon their Leader, and though I could see only the profile of his features and his body, I recognized Him at once as my Savior! The tint and radiance of His countenance were glorious to behold! There was a peace about Him which seemed sublime—it was divine!

"The city, I understood, was His. It was the City Eternal; and the people following Him were to abide there in peace and eternal happiness. But who were they? As if the Savior read my thoughts, He answered by pointing to a semicircle that then appeared above them, and on which were written in gold the words: 'These Are They Who Have Overcome The World—Who Have Truly Been Born Again!' When I awoke, it was breaking day."[146]

How Do We Overcome the World?

The Savior told President McKay that those who overcome the world will inherit the celestial kingdom. Who will overcome the world? The apostle John asked and answered this same question. "Who is he that overcometh the world, but he that believeth that Jesus is the Son of God?"[147]

We overcome the world by believing in the one who has overcome the world—Jesus! The angels of God declare, "It is finished; it is finished! The Lamb of God hath overcome and trodden the winepress alone... And then shall the angels be crowned with the glory of his might, and the saints shall be filled with his glory, and receive their inheritance and be made equal with him."[148]

Overcoming does not come as a result of our hard work. We are not crowned with the glory of our might but with the glory of Christ's might. We don't contribute to overcoming the wine-press. He did it alone. It is finished. Christ declares, "Be of good cheer; I have overcome the world."[149]

As we put our faith in Christ, we, like the apostle Paul, can say, "It is no longer I who live, but Christ who lives in me."[150] Similarly, the apostle John wrote, "Ye... have overcome... because greater is [Christ] that is in you, than he that is in the world."[151]

We can't be holy without the Holy One. We can't achieve victory without the Victorious One. We must stop trusting in the exhausting effort of self and instead place our trust in the Holy One of Hope, the God of Grace, and the Rock of Rest.

How Are We Truly Born Again?

The scriptures are clear that we must be born again to be saved in the celestial kingdom.[152] When we are born again, we have a broken heart and a contrite spirit. Being born again is having a change of heart.[153]

President Ezra Taft Benson taught, "Can human hearts be changed? Why, of course! It happens every day... The Lord works from the inside out. The world works from the outside in. The world would take people out of the slums. Christ takes the slums out of people, and then they take themselves out of the slums. The world would mold men by changing their environment. Christ changes men, who then change their environment. The world would shape human behavior, but Christ can change human nature... When you choose to follow Christ, you choose to be changed... May we be... born again."[154]

The Lord has promised to change our hearts. "I will give you a new heart and put a new spirit in you; I will remove from you your heart of stone and give you a heart of flesh."[155] When we are born again, we want to become like Christ. We want to think, feel, and act like Jesus.[156] 2 Corinthians 3:18 teaches, "As the Spirit of the Lord works within us, we become more and more like him."[157]

Have You Been Born Again?

The following analogy can be helpful in determining if we have been born again. Imagine you are holding a board with two buttons on it. If you push the first button, you will never sin again. If you push the other button, you can continue to sin. Which button would you choose to push? If you would push the button that would result in your never sinning again, you have illustrated that you don't want to sin even though you still do. If you would push the button that would allow you to continue sinning, you have not truly been born again.

Being born again does not mean we will never sin again. At the conclusion of King Benjamin's famous discourse it says that the people "all cried with one voice, saying: Yea, we believe all the words which thou hast spoken unto us; and also, we know of their surety and truth, because of the Spirit of the Lord Omnipotent, which has wrought a mighty change in us, or in our hearts, that we have no more disposition to do evil, but to do good continually."[158] These people had no more disposition to do evil and wanted to always do good.

Does this mean these people were perfect from that day forward? Of course not! Although they still continued to sin daily, their attitude toward sin had changed. They had been born again.

Why do we continue to sin even after we have been born again and justified? We commit sin because of the flesh. The Bible teaches, "For the flesh lusteth against the Spirit, and the Spirit against the flesh: and these are contrary the one to the other: so that ye cannot do the things that ye would."[159]

The apostle Paul desired to be righteous, but because of the flesh, he did things he didn't want to do, causing him to exclaim, "For we know that the law is spiritual: but I am carnal, sold under sin. For that which I do I allow not: for what I would, that do I not; but what I hate, that do I... For the good that I would I do not: but the evil which I would not, that I do... O wretched man that I am! Who shall deliver me from the body of this death?"[160]

Nephi makes a similar cry in 2 Nephi 4:17-18, "Nevertheless, notwithstanding the great goodness of the Lord, in showing me his great and marvelous works, my heart exclaimeth: O wretched man that I am! Yea, my heart sorroweth because of my flesh; my soul grieveth because of mine iniquities. I am encompassed about, because of the temptations and the sins which do so easily beset me."

Were Paul and Nephi breaking their baptismal covenants because they sinned? No! After entering the covenant of baptism, everyone continues to sin, even though they desire not to. A characteristic of one who is in a covenant relationship with Christ is not one who does not sin, but one who fights against and hates sin as did Paul and Nephi. When we are born again, we will desire to do the will of the

Lord and will strive to progress on the covenant path. We will have the desire to build the Lord's kingdom.

My Born-Again Experience

I had my born-again experience when I was fourteen. I always knew my parents knew that Jesus was the Savior of the world, that the Lord's church had been restored, and that the Book of Mormon was true, but I didn't really know these things for myself.

It was the beginning of soccer season. A few days into tryouts, one of my teammates stepped on my foot. I hoped it wasn't broken, but it hurt to walk. I couldn't even wear a shoe without experiencing pain. My parents took me to the doctor to get x-rays and the doctor confirmed my worst fears. My foot was broken. I was devastated. This injury would cause me to miss the entire season. I was feeling pretty down about my life. I couldn't play soccer. I was in pain, and I had to wear an annoying boot all the time.

Fast Sunday was a few days away, so my parents encouraged me to fast for my foot and told me they would fast with me. I agreed. When I woke up that Sunday, I said a prayer in my heart. "God, please heal my foot. I want to be able to play soccer this season. If it's Your will, please heal it. If not, Thy will be done."

The school year was about to start and my dad just happened to be giving me and my siblings back-to-school blessings after church that day. While my dad was giving me my blessing, I heard the voice of the Savior say to me, "Take off thy boot and walk." At first, I was confused, but I knew I couldn't deny what I had heard. After the blessing, I went upstairs, took off my boot and put on a pair of shoes.

I immediately knew I had been healed. I hadn't been able to put on a pair of shoes without experiencing pain since my accident, and I wasn't feeling any pain. I began to walk around my bedroom. Still, no pain. The Lord had healed my foot, and I was able to play soccer that season.

I know Jesus Christ lives and loves each and every one of us unconditionally. He gave His life so we can return to live with Him again. I know Christ's priesthood power is on the earth today and we can do all things through Christ. I know Joseph Smith was an instrument in the Lord's hands to restore Christ's church upon the earth. I know if we will ask Christ in faith, we will receive. I know I am a sinner who constantly falls short. I'm a broken, imperfect human, but I know Christ is perfect and has forgiven me of all my sins. I know that if I'm in a relationship with Him, I am perfect in Christ. I am going to the celestial kingdom, and you can too.

Now that is Good News!

CHAPTER 13
YOU ARE FORGIVEN

"I glory in my Jesus, for he hath redeemed my soul from hell."

- 2 Nephi 33:6

As this book neared completion, my dad and I pondered on what the book cover should look like. We felt the cover should include a picture of Christ. As we discussed various images of Christ, none of them felt right. Eventually, the impression came to use the painting of Christ in Gethsemane that was given to my dad in a vision[161] while he was at the Rexburg Temple. When the impression came to use this image of Christ, it felt right. This was the image God wanted for the cover of this book. My dad shared with me his journal entry about this experience, and I would like to share it with you:

I went to the Rexburg Temple on Saturday, January 25, 2020, with a group of friends to help Tracy and Richard Ward perform temple sealings for their ancestors. The Rexburg Temple had recently hung many new pieces of artwork throughout the temple. I paused and pondered at each of the new paintings in the hallways and stairwells as I made my way to the sealing rooms. On the top floor of the temple, I checked in as a part of the Tracy Ward group and was directed to a waiting room.

As I walked into the room, I saw a painting on one of the walls. I walked over to the picture. The painting was an illustration of Christ in the Garden of Gethsemane being strengthened by an angel as recorded in Luke 22:43, "And there appeared an angel unto him from heaven, strengthening him."

As I looked at the painting, I had the impression, "That's not what the painting should look like." I was initially a little shocked by the clear impression. In response, I asked, "What should the painting look like?"

I pondered on this question in the waiting room and for the next hour and a half in the sealing room. There were seven couples that were a part of the sealing session so I had a lot of time to sit in stillness and ponder on the image. As I pondered, images of what the painting should look like were brought to my mind.

The scripture in Matthew 26:39 was brought to my mind, "He went a little further, and fell on his face." Jesus was not kneeling or upright. He was face down laying on the ground. He was pressed into the ground by the sins of the world. Christ described His great pain, saying, "Which suffering caused myself, even God, the greatest of all, to tremble because of pain, and to bleed at every pore, and to suffer both body and spirit." (Doctrine and Covenants 19:18)

As I pondered further, the impression came that the angel who strengthened Jesus was not a man as was pictured in the temple waiting room. The angel was a woman. I pondered on the question, "Who was the woman who came to strengthen Jesus?" The answer came that it was Christ's mother. It was Heavenly Mother. His Mother came to strengthen Him, comfort Him, and nurture Him.

I had the thought, "When you are sick or in pain who do you want to attend to you? Who shows you the most love, concern, and care? It is your mother." I saw an image of His loving Mother lying on the ground with Him—holding Him. She was with Him. She prayed with Him.

She was in radiant white clothes. She was very close to Her Son. Her white clothes were marked red with her Son's blood. Luke 22:44 reads, "His sweat was as it were great drops of blood falling down to the ground." The blood on Her clothes was of no concern to Her.

The image panned out from a focus on Christ and His Mother to include the garden and surrounding area. Christ and His Mother were surrounded by thousands of angels. The angels were kneeling in prayer. All of the angels were women. I was surprised to see no male angels and asked, "Where are the male angels? I panned the scene in my mind and all the angels were women.

As I pondered on this scene, I had the thought that women have unique spiritual gifts to nurture, strengthen, and show compassion. The person most suited to comfort and strengthen Christ in the garden was His loving Heavenly Mother. The concourse of angels were there to pray for Him and strengthen Him. The number of angels were thousands upon thousands and more than can be numbered.

As I pondered on the images I saw, I had the impression that this was an image that Heavenly Father wanted painted. I began to ponder on the question, "Who would you like to paint it?" I had the thought that the artist should be a mother who could capture the feelings of love, compassion, and nurturing that a mother has for a child when they are in pain, sick, or injured. Christ was experiencing pain and sickness of every kind. The painter also needed to be able to paint the compassion and love of the angels who knelt surrounding Christ and His Mother in the garden.

During our family home evening lesson on Monday, April 6, 2020, my dad read the account above to our family. After reading the account, my dad shared that he received the prompting that the painting should be called "You Are Forgiven."

Initially, this seemed like an unusual name for a painting of Christ in Gethsemane. Usually, a painting would reference the place where Jesus suffered or reference a passage of scripture the image was depicting. As we discussed the name as a part of our family home evening, it became very clear why this name was given.

Christ suffered the most excruciating pain to "take away the sins of the world."[162] Christ did this so we could be forgiven. The message of Christ from Gethsemane is: "You are forgiven."

Christ's first words to countless individuals have been, "You are forgiven." Luke records a man sick of the palsy being lowered through the roof to be healed by Jesus. Jesus's first words to him were, "My friend, your sins are forgiven!"[163]

To the woman who washed His feet with her tears, Jesus declared, "Your sins are forgiven."[164]

In response to Enos's prayer, Jesus answered, "Thy sins are forgiven."[165]

When speaking to Emma Smith, the Lord said to her these glorious words, "Behold, thy sins are forgiven."[166]

When the resurrected Lord appeared to Joseph Smith in what we now call the sacred grove, His first words to the young boy were, "Joseph, my son, thy sins are forgiven."[167]

When the great Jehovah again appeared to Joseph Smith in the Kirkland Temple, He reaffirmed His prior statement saying, "Behold, your sins are forgiven you; you are clean before me; therefore, lift up your heads and rejoice."[168]

Jesus has a message He wants each of us to hear, and that message is this: "You are forgiven."

Forgiving Yourself

Christ forgives perfectly. We, on the other hand, are imperfect. Therefore, we forgive imperfectly. For most of us, the hardest person to forgive is ourselves. To fully partake of Christ's grace and forgiveness, we must forgive ourselves. We must learn to forgive ourselves as quickly and completely as the Savior does. When we don't let go of our past, we hold ourselves hostage to the guilt and pain of sin.

Christ has forgiven all of our sins, past, present, and future—all of them—100 percent. The Lord is quick to forgive and He "remember[s] [your sins] no more."[169] If you are hindered by your past, please hear these words of the Savior to you, "Your sins are forgiven. Let them trouble you no more. You are clean before Me. Please let go of anything in your past that is causing you guilt, shame, or worry. They are of no worry to Me. Don't let the past steal your present. Be of good cheer. You are forgiven. Lift up your head and rejoice!"

Becoming Friends with Jesus

One morning during our family *Come Follow Me* study, we were reading in Matthew chapter twenty-six:

"Now when Jesus was in Bethany, in the house of Simon the leper, There came unto him a woman having an alabaster box of very precious ointment, and poured it on his head, as he sat at meat. But when his disciples saw it, they had indignation, saying, To what purpose is this waste? For this ointment might have been sold for much, and given to the poor. When Jesus understood it, he said unto them, Why trouble ye the woman?… Verily I say unto you, Wheresoever this gospel shall be preached in the whole world, there shall also this, that this woman hath done, be told for a memorial of her."[170]

This verse seemed to jump from the page, "Wheresoever this gospel shall be preached in the whole world, there shall also this, that this woman hath done, be told for a memorial of her."

Why did Jesus direct that this story be shared whenever the Gospel is preached? As we discussed this question as a family, my dad said, "I have been teaching the Good News of Jesus Christ for twenty years, and I can't remember a time I have taught this story as a part of the Good News."

My dad's comment struck me. I wanted to know why Christ would want this story to be remembered and taught throughout the world, so I began pondering and praying about these verses. As I pondered and studied, I began to wonder why, with the many powerful stories Jesus could have requested to be taught with the gospel, this story would be the one Jesus requested to be shared. This story is shared with the events of Christ's atonement and crucifixion. Why were these verses important enough to be included in a chapter with such momentous events? There had to be a reason, but I wasn't seeing it yet.

A few days later, my dad and I were discussing what we had learned about this story from our individual study. We had learned that the events had taken place in the home of Simon, who had been healed of leprosy. We learned that Lazarus, whom Christ raised from the dead, had also been in the house.

"Dad," I said. "Why do you think Jesus would request the story of a woman anointing Him with ointment be shared with the gospel and not the story of Simon being healed of leprosy or the story of Lazarus being raised from the dead? Those seem like more important stories to me."

As we talked about this question, the inspiration came. Christ can heal your sickness, and He can raise you from the dead, but His greatest gift is forgiving your sins.

This woman was a sinner who was forgiven by Christ. She received His grace. She was born again by Christ's redeeming power. She heard the Good News and was changed. She received Christ's gifts of peace, love, forgiveness, and joy. She became friends with Christ and put her faith and trust in Him.

Each time we hear the story of Christ's atonement, Christ wants us to hear this woman's story. Christ wants to ensure that the gospel is not just information that is taught, but Good News that transforms. This woman's story reminds us of the power of Christ's grace and forgiveness to change us.

Christ wants every one of us to receive His gifts of forgiveness, salvation, and friendship with the joy and gratitude this woman did. She was so grateful to her Savior that she anointed Him with expensive ointment, an honor that was rare even for kings. Christ rejoices when we receive His gifts.

Some criticized Jesus for sitting with sinners and allowing sinners to touch Him. The Savior wants the story of this woman to be told so we each know He wants us close to Him and He sits with and embraces sinners.

Many have a relationship with Christ similar to their relationship with their favorite author. Even though they have read all of the author's books, they don't actually have a relationship with the author. The author is not their friend. Likewise, some have read all the books of scripture and know all about what Jesus did and said, but they don't know Him. They have a testimony that Jesus is the Son of God, but they don't believe He can be their best friend.

Jesus wants this woman's story to be told so those who hear the Good News know Jesus Christ doesn't just want us to know about Him. He wants us to know Him. He wants to be our friend. This woman was friends with Jesus. She knew Him. She loved Him. She was close to Him. The gospel of Jesus Christ is not information to learn but a relationship to strengthen.

I believe if we had asked this woman the questions we have discussed in this book, her answers would have looked like this:

Survey Questions

#1. Do you want to go to the celestial kingdom?
   Circle one: (Yes) or No

#2. If you were to die today, at the resurrection would you go to the celestial kingdom?
   Circle one: (Yes) or No or I don't know

Explain Why or Why Not?

Because I know in whom I have trusted !!!

I now invite you to complete this survey:

Survey Questions

#1. Do you want to go to the celestial kingdom?
   Circle one: Yes or No

#2. If you were to die today, at the resurrection would you go to the celestial kingdom?
   Circle one: Yes or No or I don't know

Explain Why or Why Not?

I hope you have answered "yes" to these two questions. I hope you can say with confidence, "I am saved. I am forgiven. I am going to the celestial kingdom."

"Praise the Lord for the Lord is good."[171]

You have received the Good News. Now go and share it!

"Every day, in the temple courts and from house to house, they never stopped teaching and proclaiming the good news that Jesus is the Christ." [172]

- Acts 5:42, EHV

ABOUT THE AUTHORS

Mitchell C. Taylor

Mitchell is a seventeen-year-old junior in High School and lives in Rigby, Idaho. He plays soccer for Rigby High School and loves to run. He has three siblings, one in heaven and two on earth. Mitchell has been homeschooled since the third grade.

MitchellCameronTaylor@Gmail.com

Cameron C. Taylor

Cameron, Mitchell's father, is a best-selling author of more than ten books. His favorite topic to write about is the good news of Jesus Christ. Cameron graduated with honors from Brigham Young University. He lives in Idaho with his wife and their children.

Cameron@CameronCTaylor.com
www.CameronCTaylor.com

Endnotes

1 Isaiah 1:18; Jeremiah 31:34, King James Version.
2 Doctrine and Covenants 19:16–18.
3 Nehemiah 9:17, King James Version.
4 Doctrine and Covenants 58:42.
5 1 John 1:8–9,7, King James Version.
6 Matthew 9:2, King James Version.
7 Doctrine and Covenants 110:5.
8 Luke 18:13, King James Version.
9 Matthew 14:30, King James Version.
10 Matthew 11:28–30; 3 Nephi 9:14, 22.
11 Stephen E. Robinson, *Believing Christ* (Salt Lake City: UT: Deseret Book, 1992), 24–25.
12 D. Todd Christofferson, "Justification and Sanctification," *Ensign*, June 2001.
13 3 Nephi 9:22.
14 Romans 4:5, King James Version.
15 Mark 2:17, King James Version.
16 1 Timothy 1:15, King James Version.
17 Romans 3:23 New International Version.
18 1 Nephi 10:21.
19 D. Todd Christofferson, "Justification and Sanctification," *Ensign*, June 2001.
20 Abraham Booth, *By God's Grace Alone* (London: Grace Publication Trust, 1983), 48–49.
21 C.S. Lewis, *Mere Christianity* (New York: Touchstone, 1996), 131.
22 James 2:18, King James Version.
23 Romans 6:15, King James Version.
24 Matthew 5:48, King James Version.
25 Colossians 3:10, New Century Version.
26 2 Corinthians 3:18, The Message.
27 2 Nephi 28:30.
28 Joseph Fielding Smith, *Teachings of the Prophet Joseph Smith*, Section Six 1843–44, 348.
29 Ephesians 4:13, Today's English Version.
30 D. Todd Christofferson, "Justification and Sanctification," *Ensign*, June 2001.
31 2 Nephi 2:6.
32 Alma 38:9.
33 Doctrine and Covenants 110:5.
34 Romans 3:23, New International Version.
35 1 Peter 1:3, King James Version.
36 Moroni 10:32.
37 Matthew 7:16, King James Version.
38 Hebrews 13:5, New King James Version.
39 Mark 5:28, King James Version.

40 Mark 5:35, King James Version.
41 Mark 5:36, King James Version.
42 Jeffery R. Holland, "The Laborers in the Vineyard," *General Conference,* April 2012.
43 Mark 5:36, King James Version.
44 J. Devn Cornish, "Am I Good Enough? Will I Make It?" *General Conference,* October 2016.
45 Stephen E. Robinson, *Believing Christ* (Salt Lake City, UT: Deseret Book, 1992), 74.
46 Rick Warren.
47 John 13:8, King James Version.
48 John 13:8, King James Version.
49 John 13:8, King James Version.
50 *Book of Mormon Gospel Doctrine Teacher's Manual* (Salt Lake City, UT: The Church of Jesus Christ of Latter-day Saints), 26.
51 James 2:10, King James Version.
52 Galatians 2:16, New Living Translation.
53 2 Nephi 2:5.
54 2 Nephi 2:6–9.
55 Matthew 5:16, King James Version.
56 Acts 10:38.
57 David A. Bednar, "Therefore They Hushed Their Fears," *General Conference,* April 2015.
58 Luke 7:39, King James Version.
59 Luke 7:41–43, King James Version.
60 Luke 7:44,47, King James Version
61 Dieter F. Uchtdorf, "The Gift of Grace," *General Conference,* May 2015.
62 Matthew 5:20, King James Version.
63 Matthew 9:12, King James Version.
64 3 Nephi 25:2.
65 2 Nephi 2:3.
66 Alma 38:14.
67 John 4:13–14, King James Version.
68 Jeremiah 2:13, New Century Version.
69 Matthew 5:6, King James Version.
70 2 Nephi 26:9.
71 Bruce R. McConkie, "The Probationary Test of Mortality," Address given at University of Utah Institute, January 10, 1982, p. 11.
72 Shayne M. Bowen, "Because I Live, Ye Shall Live Also," *General Conference,* October 2012.
73 Moroni 8:22.
74 Bruce R. McConkie, "The Salvation of Little Children," *Ensign,* April 1977.
75 Doctrine and Covenants 137:10.
76 2 Nephi 2:8.
77 2 Nephi 2:8.

78 2 Nephi 31:19, Alma 7:14, Alma 34:18, Doctrine and Covenants 133:47.
79 2 Nephi 2:8.
80 2 Nephi 2:8.
81 Alma 26:10–36.
82 2 Nephi 31:19.
83 Dieter F. Uchtdorf, "Your Potential, Your Privilege," *General Conference,* April 2011.
84 M. Russell Ballard, "God Is at the Helm," *General Conference,* November 2015.
85 Doctrine and Covenants 88:33.
86 M. Russell Ballard, "God Is at the Helm," *General Conference,* November 2015.
87 M. Russell Ballard, "God Is at the Helm," *General Conference,* November 2015.
88 "Master the Tempest Is Raging," Hymns, no 105.
89 Matthew 20:1–15, King James Version.
90 Jeffery R. Holland, "Be Ye Therefore Perfect-Eventfully," *General Conference,* October 2017.
91 Dieter F. Ucthdorf, "The Gift of Grace", *General Conference,* April 2015.
92 Doctrine and Covenants 130:19.
93 Revelation 7:9, King James Version, Revelation 7:10, Good News Translation.
94 Doctrine and Covenants 108:8.
95 1 Corinthians 15:22, King James Version.
96 D. Todd Christofferson, "Justification and Sanctification," *Ensign,* June 2001.
97 Numbers 21:6-9, King James Version.
98 1 Nephi 17:41, Alma 33:20.
99 Max Lucado, Tricia Goyer, *3:16 The Numbers of Hope* (Nashville, TN: Thomas Nelson, 2007), 96.
100 John 3:14–17.
101 Alma 37:44–47.
102 Matthew 11:28-30, King James Version.
103 Psalm 84:5, New Living Translation.
104 Hebrews 10:18, New Living Translation.
105 2 Nephi 2:27.
106 Dieter F. Uchtdorf, "The Gift of Grace," *General Conference,* April 2015.
107 Isaiah 55:1, King James Version.
108 Isaiah 55:1, King James Version.
109 Isaiah 55:1, Good News Translation.
110 Matthew 25:35, King James Version.
111 Matthew 25:36, King James Version.
112 Ephesians 1:7, Contemporary English Version.
113 Jeffrey R. Holland, "Be Ye Therefore Perfect—Eventually," *General Conference,* October 2017.
114 Hebrews 12:2.

115 Dale G. Renlund, "Latter-day Saints Keep on Trying." *General Conference,* April 2015.

116 Joseph Fielding Smith, *Teachings of the Prophet Joseph Smith,* Section Six 1843–44, 348.

117 D. Todd Christofferson, "The Living Bread Which Came Down from Heaven," *General Conference,* October 2017.

118 Matthew 9:12, King James Version.

119 Matthew 9:13, Contemporary English Version.

120 Luke 15:2, King James Version.

121 Luke 15:4–7, New International Version.

122 Alma 38:14.

123 Russell M. Nelson, "We Can Do Better and Be Better," *General Conference,* April 2019.

124 Luke 15:8–10, King James Version.

125 Luke 15:17–28, New International Version.

126 Luke 15:21, New International Version.

127 Luke 15:29, New Heart English Bible.

128 1 John 1:8–9,7, King James Version.

129 Luke 18:9, King James Version.

130 Luke 18:10–14, King James Version.

131 1 Timothy 1:15, King James Version.

132 2 Nephi 4:17–19.

133 2 Nephi 4:34,30,32,33.

134 James L. Ferrell, *The Hidden Christ* (Salt Lake City, UT: Deseret Book, 2009), 23.

135 Stephen E. Robinson, *Believing Christ* (Salt Lake City, UT: Deseret Book, 1992), 90–92.

136 Dieter F. Uchtdorf, "The Gift of Grace," *General Conference,* April 2015.

137 Ken Radke, *But Grace Is Enough* (Fort Washington, PA: Christian Literature Crusade, 1991), 21–25.

138 Galatians 2:16, 20-21, King James Version.

139 Matthew 9:2, English Standard Version; Mark 2:5, English Standard Version

140 Luke 19:9–10, King James Version.

141 Moroni 8:23.

142 2 Nephi 25:23.

143 Matthew 28:20, New King James Version, Hebrews 13:5, New King James Version.

144 Zephaniah 3:17, GOD'S WORD Translation.

145 Russell M. Nelson, "Drawing the Power of Jesus Christ into Our Lives," *General Conference,* April 2017.

146 David O. McKay, Clare Middlemiss, *Cherished Experiences from the Writings of President David O. McKay* (Salt Lake City, UT: Deseret Book, 1955), 101–102.

147 1 John 5:5, King James Version.

148 Doctrine and Covenants 88:106-107.

149 John 16:33, King James Version.

150 Galatians 2:20, English Standard Version.

151 1 John 4:4, King James Version.

152 "If ye are not born again ye cannot inherit the kingdom of heaven." Alma 7:14.

"And the Lord said unto me: Marvel not that all mankind, yea, men and women, all nations, kindreds, tongues and people, must be born again; yea, born of God, changed from their carnal and fallen state, to a state of righteousness, being redeemed of God." Mosiah 27:25.

"Preach unto all, both old and young, both bond and free yea...cry unto them that they must repent and be born again." Alma 5:49.

"Ye must be born again...and be cleansed by blood, even the blood of mine Only Begotten." Moses 6:59.

"Except a man be born again, he cannot see the kingdom of God." John 3:3, King James Version.

153 Alma 5:12–14.

154 Ezra Taft Benson, "Born of God," *General Conference,* October 1985.

155 Ezekiel 36:26, New International Version.

156 Philippians 2:5, Colossians 3:15, Colossians 3:17.

157 2 Corinthians 3:18, The Living Bible.

158 Mosiah 5:2.

159 Galatians 5:17, King James Version.

160 Romans 7:14,15,19,24, King James Version.

161 "And it shall come to pass in the last days, saith God, I will pour out of my Spirit upon all flesh: and your sons and your daughters shall prophesy, and your young men shall see visions, and your old men shall dream dreams." Acts 2:17, King James Version.

162 John 1:29, The Passion Translation.

163 Luke 5:20 Living Bible.

164 Luke 7:48, New King James Version.

165 Enos 1:5.

166 Doctrine and Covenants 25:3.

167 1832 account of the first vision.

168 Doctrine and Covenants 110:5.

169 Doctrine and Covenants 58:42.

170 Matthew 26:6–13, King James Version.

171 Psalm 135:3, King James Version.

172 Acts 5:42, Evangelical Heritage Version.

The Way of Aloha: Lanaʻi

"Best book ever! I love this book!!! It truly changed my life! I like it so much tha I have bought 10 of them for my family!"
-Jon Pabst

The Way of Aloha: Molokaʻi

"I absolutely loved it! I felt the Spirit many times. Especially when they there chanting for protection against the invading Tahitians. The Father Damien story has inspired me as well. Thank you for being who you are."
-Rick Tompot

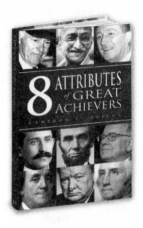

8 Attributes of Great Achievers

"I thought *8 Attributes of Great Achievers* was an excellent read with interesting and deep stories. I enjoyed it more than any book I've read in quite a while. I had a hard time putting it down."

-MARK DENNISON

Twelve Paradoxes of the Gospel

"Cameron's strong faith comes through in his book and there is no doubt he was inspired to write it."

-LOU HOLTZ, Former Head Football Coach, *University of Notre Dame*

Preserve, Protect & Defend

"*Preserve, Protect & Defend* was a great read, filled with the spirit all through. No man wrote it, God did. I'm 61 and cried all through it. Thank you for sharing your talents."

-S. DEAN CHAPPELL

8 Attributes of Great Achievers Volume II

"I am writing to share with you how much I enjoyed reading your book. I was deeply touched, encouraged, inspired, and challenged. I laughed and I cried. Every day I have been sharing with my husband what I am learning, and I keep on saying 'This is such an amazing book!!!'"

-CORA BUSHEY

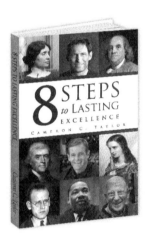

8 Steps to Lasting Excellence

"Phenomenal. I devoured this book in 3 days, as the stories, lessons, and insights proved amazing."

-CHRISTOPHER WILD

Does Your Bag Have Holes?

"Cameron was meant to write, and he does so beautifully. He writes with humor, insight, and profound wisdom. I came across so many different stories that I wanted to scan/type in and share. They're that amazing."

-JOI SIGERS